KenKen®
FOR
DUMMIES®

**by Tetsuya Miyamoto and
KenKen Puzzle, LLC**

WILEY
Wiley Publishing, Inc.

KenKen® For Dummies®

Published by
Wiley Publishing, Inc.
111 River Street
Hoboken, NJ 07030-5774

www.wiley.com

Copyright © 2010 by Wiley Publishing, Inc., Indianapolis, Indiana

Published by Wiley Publishing, Inc., Indianapolis, Indiana

Published simultaneously in Canada

For general information on our other products and services, please contact our Customer Care Department within the U.S. at 877-762-2974, outside the U.S. at 317-572-3993, or fax 317-572-4002.

For technical support, please visit www.wiley.com/techsupport.

Wiley also publishes its books in a variety of electronic formats. Some content that appears in print may not be available in electronic books.

Library of Congress Control Number: 2010930966

ISBN: 978-0-470-61656-7

Manufactured in the United States of America

10 9 8 7 6 5 4 3 2 1

WILEY

Publisher's Acknowledgments

We're proud of this book; please send us your comments at http://dummies.custhelp.com. For other comments, please contact our Customer Care Department within the U.S. at 877-762-2974, outside the U.S. at 317-572-3993, or fax 317-572-4002.

Some of the people who helped bring this book to market include the following:

Acquisitions and Editorial

Project Editor: Sarah Faulkner

Acquisitions Editor: Tracy Boggier

Copy Editor: Amanda M. Langferman

Editorial Manager: Christine Meloy Beck

Editorial Assistants: Jennette ElNaggar, Rachelle S. Amick

Senior Editorial Assistant: David Lutton

Cartoons: Rich Tennant
(www.the5thwave.com)

Composition Services

Project Coordinator: Kristie Rees

Layout and Graphics: Mark Pinto, Erin Zeltner

Proofreaders: Laura Bowman, Lauren Mandelbaum

Publishing and Editorial for Consumer Dummies

Diane Graves Steele, Vice President and Publisher, Consumer Dummies

Kristin Ferguson-Wagstaffe, Product Development Director, Consumer Dummies

Ensley Eikenburg, Associate Publisher, Travel

Kelly Regan, Editorial Director, Travel

Publishing for Technology Dummies

Andy Cummings, Vice President and Publisher, Dummies Technology/General User

Composition Services

Debbie Stailey, Director of Composition Services

Contents at a Glance

Introduction

● ●

*T*he Japanese word *Ken* means "wisdom," and the name *KenKen* translates to "wisdom squared." The puzzles in this book are designed to test and expand your wisdom by forcing you to call on your powers of math and logic. If you're afraid your logic is rusty from lack of use, have no fear — by the time you work a handful of these puzzles, the rust will fall away. You'll feel your brain matter getting primed for even greater challenges, and your biggest problem will be setting down the book!

If you haven't worked a KenKen puzzle before — if you're looking at this book because you've heard about this KenKen craze and want to know why the puzzles are so popular — rest assured that you can learn the rules in a matter of minutes. The rules themselves are very simple. The challenges posed by the KenKen puzzle grid, on the other hand, can be surprisingly difficult.

For the KenKen pros out there, this book offers a hearty menu of puzzles that range from easy to treacherous. With more than 250 puzzles to choose from, you should have no trouble feeding your KenKen addiction.

About This Book

I created the KenKen puzzle in 2004 when I was working as a teacher in Japan. I wanted to help my students improve their thinking skills in a new way. The puzzle fits perfectly into the "teaching without teaching" method I use in the classroom; my curriculum includes a set amount of time during which students challenge themselves with KenKen puzzles (with no assistance from me or any other instructor).

Although KenKen puzzles have been available to the public in Japan since 2006, Western audiences didn't even know what they were until 2008. (In Japan, KenKen puzzles are called Kashikku Naru puzzles, which translates to "the puzzle that makes you smarter.") The response to KenKen has been so strong and so immediate that puzzlers are demanding — and receiving — access to more and more puzzles all the time.

That's where *KenKen For Dummies* comes in. Although you can now find KenKen puzzles online, in magazines, and in some daily newspapers, only a book like this — with so many puzzles to choose from at varying levels of difficulty — can satisfy everyone from the KenKen novice to the puzzle lover who just can't get enough.

Conventions Used in This Book

In Part I, I explain the rules of KenKen and offer examples of how to solve a puzzle grid. In addition, I direct you to online resources where you can find more information and more puzzles to solve. The Web addresses I provide appear in `monofont` so they stand out and are easy to find when you go back to the chapter.

Keep in mind that when the book printed, some Web addresses may have needed to break onto a second line of text. In that situation, I didn't add any symbols (such as hyphens) to indicate the break. Simply type in the Web address as if the break didn't exist, and you'll find the resource you need!

Part II features the puzzles themselves, which are classified according to their level of difficulty: easy, tricky, and treacherous. The Kenerator, which is the computer program that creates KenKen puzzles, assesses the difficulty of each puzzle by evaluating a number of factors that affect the ease or difficulty of a puzzle. Your results may vary, but the Kenerator's assessments are generally accurate. If you have just a few minutes to work a puzzle while you're drinking your morning coffee, stick with the easy ones. When you have more time to spare and feel comfortable with the puzzle rules, try out some of the tricky puzzles. Only when you're willing to devote some serious time and brain energy to the effort should you tackle a treacherous grid!

What You're Not to Read

You don't have to read this book from cover to cover to follow what's going on. If you're an experienced KenKen puzzler, feel free to skip Chapter 1. If the easy puzzles are too easy for you, skip those, too. And if the treacherous puzzles prove to be too tough, ignore them — at least until you build your skills and are ready for the challenge.

No matter what level KenKen solver you are, you'll find what you're looking for in this book. All you need is a pencil and your mind to get started!

Foolish Assumptions

The only assumption I made about you as I wrote this book is that you're in one way, shape, or form interested in KenKen puzzles. You may be a beginner, a puzzle mastermind, or somewhere in between.

Rest assured that I don't assume anything about your KenKen experience — or your experience with other types of puzzles. You don't need to have a PhD in Sudoku or be a crossword fanatic to enjoy this book. If you can do basic math — addition, subtraction, multiplication, and division — you can work these puzzles. And if you've never touched a KenKen puzzle before, Chapter 1 provides all the information you need to get started.

How This Book Is Organized

The bulk of this book is devoted to what you were looking for when you bought it: puzzles (and their solutions, of course). The following sections show you how the book is structured so you can dive in wherever your mind takes you.

Part 1: Navigating the KenKen Grid

This part is where you find the basics of KenKen. If you're already working these puzzles on a regular basis, you can skip this part altogether. But if you haven't touched a KenKen puzzle before, this part shows you everything you need to know to get started: the rules of the game, examples of how to tackle a puzzle, and tips for when you get stuck.

Part 11: KenKen Puzzlemania

This part contains more than 250 KenKen puzzles at various levels of difficulty. The puzzles are organized according to size. Within the different sizes, the easiest puzzles come first, and some fairly tricky puzzles follow. I save the downright treacherous ones for last. The difficulty level of each puzzle appears on the page so you know what to expect.

Part III: Satisfying Your Need to Be Right: Solutions

With KenKen, you generally know when you've worked a grid correctly; after all, each puzzle has only one solution. But if you enjoy the satisfaction of checking your solutions, you can find them in Part III. And if a particular grid threatens to trigger a migraine, the solutions are available for stress relief, as well. I trust that you'll use them only in extreme cases; otherwise, you rob yourself of the joy that comes from finally solving the toughest of puzzles.

Icons Used in This Book

In Chapter 1, you'll notice I use the following two icons in the margins to help you navigate the text:

When you see this icon, you know that the text next to it contains a helpful hint for solving a KenKen puzzle.

This icon points out information you want to tuck into your mental filing cabinet for future use. Believe me: It'll come in handy as you make your way through the puzzles in this book.

Where to Go from Here

What you do now depends entirely on you. If you're new to KenKen, I recommend that you cozy up with Part I before putting pencil to paper in Part II. If you're already familiar with how these puzzles work, feel free to jump directly into the good stuff: the puzzles themselves in Part II.

My only rule is that you can't go directly to Part III! But I assume that because you've taken the time to read this Introduction, you're not going to spoil your fun by looking at the solutions before making an earnest effort to solve the puzzles yourself.

Part I

Navigating the KenKen Grid

"It's a game called KenKen. It keeps me sharp."

In this part . . .

The rules of KenKen are simple, and, to help you get started, I lay them out in this part. But just because the rules are simple doesn't mean the puzzles are always easy to solve! For this reason, I offer several different examples of how to approach filling in the KenKen grid, starting with the easiest kind of puzzle you'll see and moving on to more challenging examples. After you read Part I, you'll be poised and ready for what awaits you in Part II: the puzzles themselves.

Chapter 1

Working a KenKen Puzzle

*H*ere's a fun fact about KenKen puzzles: Today they're all computer generated. I originally created them by hand, but for convenience and mass-marketing, we use a software program called *the Kenerator,* which I helped develop using artificial intelligence techniques. The Kenerator cranks out the puzzles and checks each one to make sure it has one and only one solution. So when you get stuck on a grid, make sure you curse the Kenerator — not me. (I'll gladly take credit for the enjoyment you derive from this book, however.)

Truth be told, I myself sometimes get stuck on a grid, which is probably why I'm such a big fan of KenKen. Although I'm pretty good at solving puzzles, my logic truly gets a workout when I work on some of the more challenging grids (like the treacherous ones in this book).

In this chapter, I spell out the rules of KenKen puzzles and provide some strategies you can use when you're getting started (or when you find yourself stuck on a particular grid). Along the way, I offer several examples of how to solve a grid because the best way to explain the rules of KenKen is to show them in action.

As an added bonus, I also offer you a few great KenKen resources you can use to satisfy your KenKen cravings even when you don't have this book in hand.

Getting Familiar with the Grid

If you've ever worked on or seen a Sudoku puzzle grid, the format of a KenKen grid will look familiar. (Keep in mind that KenKen isn't derived from Sudoku; although they're both logic puzzles, the rules of one don't apply to the other.) Figure 1-1 shows an example of the smallest KenKen grid: one that has three rows and three columns.

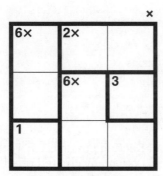

Figure 1-1: A 3 × 3 KenKen grid.

You also find KenKen grids that are 4 × 4 (four rows, four columns), 5 × 5, 6 × 6, 7 × 7, 8 × 8, and 9 × 9. For each size grid, your solution needs to include as many numbers as there are rows or columns. For example:

- With a 3 × 3 grid, you use the numbers 1 through 3 in your solution.

- With a 5 × 5 grid, you use the numbers 1 through 5 in your solution.

- With a 9 × 9 grid, you use the numbers 1 through 9 in your solution.

To solve a KenKen puzzle, your job is to place each of your allowable numbers (1 to 3, 1 to 4, 1 to 5, and so on) on the grid only once in each row and once in each column. So, for example, if you're working on a 3 × 3 grid, you have to include 1, 2, and 3 in each row and 1, 2, and 3 in each column, and you can't have repeating numbers in any row or column.

The following sections take you through the main elements of KenKen grids and show you how to work through them.

Spotting cages and target numbers

To *solve* a puzzle — to figure out which number to write in which box in each row and column — you have to do simple arithmetic: addition, subtraction, multiplication, and division. No need to stress out; the grid itself tells you which math operations you must use.

Take a look at Figure 1-1. Notice that some of the grid lines are thicker than others. The thick lines create what are called *cages.* All the boxes surrounded by a thick line are part of a single cage.

In the upper-left corner of every cage, you find a number that's (usually) followed by a math symbol: +, –, ×, or ÷. The number is called the *target number,* and the math symbol indicates how you have to reach the target number for that cage. For example, if you see *5+* in the upper-left corner of a cage containing three boxes, you need to find three numbers that add up to 5. If you see *3÷* in a cage with two boxes, you need to find two numbers that, when one is divided into the other, equal 3.

As you work your way through each cage, you need to keep in mind a couple of important rules:

- ✔ **You can repeat numbers within a cage as long as doing so doesn't result in repeating numbers within a row or column.** For example, say you're working on an *L*-shaped cage that contains three boxes in a 4 × 4 grid. If your target number is 6+, your solution could be either 1 + 2 + 3 or 1 + 1 + 4.

- ✔ **You don't have to place numbers in mathematical order within the cage.** For example, say you have a horizontal cage with two boxes, and the target number is 2–. If your solution is 3 – 1, the 3 doesn't have to appear on the left and the 1 on the right; they could be the other way around.

Look at Figure 1-1 again. The grid contains five cages:

- ✔ In the upper left, a cage contains two boxes and the target number 6×.

- ✔ In the upper right, a cage contains two boxes and the target number 2×.

✔ In the bottom right, a cage contains three boxes and the target number 6×.

✔ The remaining two cages consist of single boxes: one with the target number 1 and one with the target number 3. Note that the target numbers in these cages don't include math symbols.

So what does each target number tell you? Start with the simplest cages — the ones that contain only one box each. These one-box cages are called *singleton cages,* and the target number shown in each box is the solution for that cage. (That's why no math function is indicated.) You solve the two singleton cages in Figure 1-1 by writing *1* in the box in the lower-left corner and *3* in the box in the middle of the far-right column. Pretty easy so far, right?

The other three cages in the example require a bit more thought than the singleton cages. Each of the three remaining cages contains the math symbol ×, which means you have to do multiplication to arrive at each of your solutions. Here's what you need to do:

✔ In the upper-left corner, find two numbers that equal the target number 6 when multiplied together.

✔ In the upper-right corner, find two numbers that equal the target number 2 when multiplied together.

✔ In the bottom-right corner, find three numbers that equal the target number 6 when multiplied together.

Keeping in mind that your only number options in this puzzle are 1, 2, and 3 (because it's a 3×3 grid), the solutions should be pretty easy:

✔ The only two numbers that can be multiplied to equal 6 are 2 and 3.

✔ The only two numbers that can be multiplied to equal 2 are 1 and 2.

✔ The only three numbers that can be multiplied to equal 6 are 1, 2, and 3.

Simple, huh? All you have to do is write those numbers in the boxes. But which number goes in which box within a cage? Remember that you can't repeat numbers in a row or in a column. So the solution to the KenKen grid isn't done when your math calculations are complete. You still have to decide which number goes in which box.

Assigning a number to each box

Before your solution is complete, you have to figure out which number goes in which box in each cage. For example, in the cage in the upper-left corner of Figure 1-1, which box gets the 2 and which box gets the 3?

When answering a question like this one, try out this strategy:

✔ **Complete every part of the grid that you can work with certainty.** If you can't yet say with certainty how to place any of the numbers within a given cage, move on to another cage.

✔ **If you've filled in every number you're certain about and can't move forward, write down all the number possibilities for the boxes that remain and consider how each possibility affects the rest of the grid.**

The example in Figure 1-1 is easy enough that the first method is all you need to get the solution. (I tackle the second method in the section "Developing Your Strategy" later in this chapter.)

Here's how I'd start to solve the puzzle in Figure 1-1: The singleton cage that contains the number 3 tells me that 3 can't appear again in the right column or in the middle row. The singleton cage that contains the number 1 tells me that the left column and the bottom row can't contain another 1.

Combine these facts with the need to place 1, 2, and 3 within the cage on the bottom right. You know that 1 can't appear again in the bottom row, which means 1 must go in the middle box of the grid. You also know that 3 can't appear again in the right column, which means 3 must go in the middle of the bottom row. That leaves only 2 for the bottom-right corner. Now your grid looks like Figure 1-2.

×

6×	2×	
	6× *1*	3 *3*
1 *1*	*3*	*2*

Figure 1-2: A partial solution to the sample puzzle in Figure 1-1.

With this much of the puzzle complete, figuring out the rest should be pretty easy. The box in the first column and second row must be 2 so that you don't have any repeating numbers in that row. With that number in place, you don't even have to look at target numbers and math functions; you can simply fill in the rest of the grid to avoid repeating numbers in the three columns. When you do, your solution is complete and accurate (see Figure 1-3).

×

6× *3*	2× *2*	*1*
2	6× *1*	3 *3*
1 *1*	*3*	*2*

Figure 1-3: The complete solution to the puzzle in Figure 1-1.

Each grid has a unique solution, meaning it can't be solved in more than one way. (The Kenerator makes certain of that!) If you ever find yourself debating between two puzzle solutions that seem equally valid to you, take a step back and look for your mistake. Two solutions simply aren't possible.

Walking through an easy example

Figure 1-4 shows a 4 × 4 grid that isn't too tough to solve (in fact, it's considered *easy* according to the difficulty-rating conventions I use in this book — check out the Introduction for more details). To give you a bit more practice with easier puzzles before you move on to something more complex, I walk you through the steps I'd take to solve the puzzle in this section. Keep in mind that you need to place the numbers 1 through 4 in each row and each column.

$+ - × ÷$

1—		1	2÷
3—	12×		
	3—	6×	4+
2			

Figure 1-4: An example of an easy 4 × 4 grid.

Here's one way to move toward the solution to the puzzle in Figure 1-4:

1. **Fill in the singleton cages in the top and bottom rows.**

   These freebees are your gifts from the Kenerator. (It's a generous little computer program.)

2. **You know that the only numbers that work in the cage with the target number 6× are 3 and 2, so fill in that cage next.**

   Because 2 already appears in the bottom row, it's easy to figure out where the numbers have to go within this cage: 2 goes in the third row, and 3 goes in the fourth.

3. **To complete the third column, write *4* in the box in the second row.**

   In doing so, you help solve the cage with the target number 12×. The remaining box in that cage must be 3.

   At this point, your grid looks like the one in Figure 1-5.

Figure 1-5: A partial solution to the sample puzzle in Figure 1-4.

4. **Look at the cage on the left side of the grid with 3– as the target number, and fill in its solution.**

   The only solution for that target number in this puzzle is 4 – 1. The 4 that's already in the second row dictates the number order here; 1 must go in the second row and 4 in the third row.

5. **With all but one number placed in the first column, you can complete that column by writing *3* in the top-left box.**

   Figure 1-6 shows your progress up to this point.

6. **Take a look at the cage with 2÷ as its target number, and fill in its solution.**

   You know that two solutions are possible for this cage: 4 ÷ 2 or 2 ÷ 1. But with the number 1 already appearing in both the first and second rows, you can eliminate 2 ÷ 1 as a possibility. (You can't place the 1 anywhere in the cage without repeating it in one of the rows.) The only solution is 4 ÷ 2. And the only number placement that works is 4 in the first row and 2 in the second; otherwise, you'd have repeating 4s in the second row.

+ − × ÷

1− 3		1 /	2÷
3− 1	12× 3	4	
4	3−	6× 2	4+
2 2		3	

Figure 1-6: Halfway to the solution to the puzzle in Figure 1-4.

7. **With all but one number complete in the first row, write *2* in the second column to complete the 1− cage.**

Figure 1-7 shows where your puzzle stands.

+ − × ÷

1− 3	2	1 /	2÷ 4
3− 1	12× 3	4	2
4	3−	6× 2	4+
2 2		3	

Figure 1-7: Rounding third base toward the solution to the puzzle in Figure 1-4.

8. **You know that 3 + 1 has to complete the fourth column (in the 4+ cage); fill in the numbers so you don't repeat 3 in the bottom row.**

9. **Fill in the remaining 3– cage by completing the bottom two rows: 1 goes in the third row and 4 in the fourth.**

You don't need any guesswork to solve this puzzle. You've filled in each cage with certainty, and the end result is the unique solution shown in Figure 1-8.

Figure 1-8: The complete solution to the puzzle in Figure 1-4.

Developing Your Strategy

As I note earlier in this chapter, you use two basic strategies to fill in a KenKen grid: completing any boxes you can fill in with certainty and considering possibilities for the rest of the boxes. The first method is pretty straightforward, as the 4 × 4 grid example in the section "Walking through an easy example" demonstrates.

In this section, I offer tips for how to approach more complex puzzles in which you run up against uncertainty, but, believe it or not, none of these tips involves guessing. Because each KenKen grid has a logical, unique solution, guesswork is never the quickest way to solve it.

Considering candidates

When you run out of solutions that you're certain about within a grid, what you're left with are possibilities, or *candidates*. Here are two keys to moving forward when you get to this point in a puzzle:

- ✔ Consider how possible solutions in one cage interact with possible solutions in other cages.

- ✔ Use a pencil as you consider possible solutions.

Obviously, these two guidelines are intertwined. The pencil allows you to write number candidates in each box of the grid (and erase them when you discover they're wrong). Doing so helps you check possibilities for one box against possibilities for another, which can transform an uncertainty into a certainty.

The best way to demonstrate what I mean is to show you an example. Take a look at the slightly more challenging grid I show you in Figure 1-9.

Figure 1-9: A tricky 5 × 5 grid that presents a greater challenge.

Just a reminder that because this puzzle is a 5 × 5 grid, your goal is to fill in each row and each column with the numbers 1 through 5. Begin by filling in the easy stuff first: The Kenerator offers you one singleton cage here, in the bottom-right corner. Fill it in — it's free!

Hmmm . . . now what? With just one number given and ten empty cages staring you in the face, how do you proceed?

For the sake of clarity, I take a fairly linear approach to this grid to show you which possibilities you need to consider as you move toward your solution. Start at the top left and work your way across and down, considering what each cage tells you.

Note that you can also start solving the puzzle in Figure 1-9 using a less-linear approach — by figuring out which target numbers have only one possible solution. You can do so in a variety of ways, but you may want to look first at the most unusual target numbers. In this puzzle, consider 60× first and see where it leads you. If you get stumped, move through the more-linear approach I outline in this section.

1– cage

This cage has four possible solutions (5 – 4, 4 – 3, 3 – 2, and 2 – 1). With so many options, your best option is to skip this cage for the moment. After all, you're bound to find other cages that offer fewer possibilities.

10+ cage

Because more than one combination of numbers is possible for this cage (5 + 4 + 1 and 5 + 3 + 2), keep it simmering a bit longer, too. (Note that because all the boxes in this cage appear within the same row, you can't repeat any numbers within it, which allows you to eliminate the possibility 4 + 3 + 3.)

5× cage

Aha! Only one possibility works here: 5 × 1 × 1. Because you have an *L*-shaped cage, using two 1s is acceptable. And because the 1s can't appear in the same row or the same column, you know exactly where the numbers in this cage belong: 1 and 5 in the second row, 1 in the third row. Fill 'em in!

5+ cage (second row)

With the 5× cage solved, you eliminate the possibility of using
4 + 1 to solve this cage; the 1 can't fit in either position without
repeating itself in a row. Therefore, your only solution is 3 + 2,
but you don't yet know in which order the 3 and 2 need to go.

How do you remind yourself that you're close to a solution
without taking an unnecessary guess? Write the number candidates in each box of the cage (in pencil, of course). Figure
1-10 shows you what I mean.

Figure 1-10: Noting number candidates within a cage.

60× cage

This target number is the most unusual one in the puzzle,
and its solution is unique: The only possibility is $5 \times 4 \times 3$.
Because you've filled in the 5× cage already, you know that
the 5 can't go in either position in the second row; thus, it has
to go in the third row. But at the moment, you can't be certain
which box in the second row should house the 4 and which
one should house the 3. Again, note your candidates in those
boxes (see Figure 1-11).

+ − × ÷

1−		10+			
5× *1*	*5*	5+ *2 3*	60× *3 4*		*3 4*
1−	*1*	*2 3*	*5*		5+
	10×		2÷		
7+					1 *1*

Figure 1-11: Marking additional candidates.

At this point, although you can't solve this cage completely, you can solve the 5+ cage to its left. How? Look at the number candidates you've written in the second row of Figure 1-11. You know with certainty that the number 3 has to appear in either the fourth or fifth column. Therefore, it can't appear in the third column. With confidence, you can now write *2* in the second row and *3* below it to complete the 5+ cage.

1– cage (both of them)

Thanks to the 5× cage you've already filled in, you know that neither of these solutions can include the number 1, so you can eliminate 2 – 1. But, at the moment, 3 – 2, 4 – 3, and 5 – 4 are still possibilities in both cages, so your best option is to go on to the next cage and come back to this one later.

5+ cage (third row)

The option 4 + 1 is out because you can't place 1 in this cage without repeating it in the same column, so your solution is definitely 3 + 2. The order of the numbers is certain, too, because you can't repeat 3 in the third row. Fill in the solution (see Figure 1-12).

+ − × ÷

1−		10+			
5× *1*	*5*	5+ *2*	60× *3* *4*	*3*	*4*
1−	*1*	*3*	*5*	5+ *2*	
	10×		2÷		*3*
7+				1 *1*	

Figure 1-12: Inching closer to the solution to the puzzle in Figure 1-9.

Take a close look at the grid in Figure 1-12. Do you see how solving the 5+ cage in the far-right column allows you to solve, with certainty, the 60× cage? With 3 already in the fifth column, you know that the 3 in the 60× cage has to go in the fourth column. Erase the candidates, and write the solutions!

At this point, you can complete the fifth column by writing 5 in the upper-right corner. If you think back to the possibilities for completing the 10+ cage (5 + 4 + 1 and 5 + 3 + 2), you now know with certainty that 5 + 4 + 1 is the solution because you can't place 3 in either of the positions remaining in that cage. But which box gets the 4, and which box gets the 1? You don't know for certain, yet, so just note these candidates in their possible boxes. Your grid now looks like the one in Figure 1-13.

Before you move on, you can complete the third row by writing 4 in the box in the first column. And because you can't repeat the number 3 in the fourth row, you know the solution to the vertical 1− cage is 5 − 4; so write 5 in the box in the fourth row.

+ − × ÷

1−		10+ *1 4*	*1 4*	*5*
5× *1*	*5*	5+ *2*	60× *3*	*4*
1−	*1*	*3*	*5*	5+ *2*
	10×		2÷	*3*
7+			1 *1*	

Figure 1-13: Halfway to the solution to the puzzle in Figure 1-9.

10× cage

The only possible solution to this cage is $5 \times 2 \times 1$. Because the second column already contains a 5 and a 1, you know with certainty that the second-column position in this cage requires the 2. And because the bottom row already has a 1, the 5 must assume the bottom-row position in this cage; the remaining box must be 1. Figure 1-14 shows your progress so far.

You can now go back and solve the 10+ cage with certainty. You know that the 4 in that cage must appear in the third column, which puts the 1 in the fourth column. Erase the candidates, and fill in the solutions.

2÷ cage

You can't solve this one with $2 \div 1$ because 1 can't fit in either position of this cage. Therefore, your only possibility is $4 \div 2$. (The other way to arrive at this conclusion is just to look at the numbers already appearing in the fourth column; 4 and 2 are the only remaining possibilities.) Because you already have 2 in the fourth row, you know that 4 goes in the fourth row and 2 goes in the fifth (see Figure 1-15).

+ − × ÷

1−		10+		
1	4	1	4	5
5×	5	5+ 2	60× 3	4
1				
1− 4	1	3	5	5+ 2
5	10× 2	1	2÷	3
7+		5		1 1

Figure 1-14: Only a few boxes to go before you're done with the puzzle in Figure 1-9.

+ − × ÷

1−		10+		
		4	1	5
5× 1	5	5+ 2	60× 3	4
1− 4	1	3	5	5+ 2
5	10× 2	1	2÷ 4	3
7+		5	2	1 1

Figure 1-15: In the home stretch of the solution to the puzzle in Figure 1-9.

7+ cage

The solution to this cage must be 3 + 4. The number placement is also certain: 3 must appear in the first column and 4 in the second.

You can now jump back to the top left of the puzzle and fill in the very first cage you considered: 1–. The number 2 goes in the first column, and 3 goes in the second.

Voilà! Your solution is complete (see Figure 1-16). You made absolutely no guesses along the way; your logic guided you from the many possibilities toward the unique solutions for each cage.

+ − × ÷

1– 2	3	10+ 4	1	5
5× 1	5	5+ 2	60× 3	4
1– 4	1	3	5	5+ 2
5	10× 2	1	2÷ 4	3
7+ 3	4	5	2	1 1

Figure 1-16: Complete solution to the puzzle in Figure 1-9.

Getting unstuck

Every puzzle-doer meets his match at one time or another; you know what I'm talking about — the puzzle that refuses to be solved. I wish I could say you'll never meet a KenKen puzzle that causes you grief, but you will. I certainly have.

So what do you do when you're truly stumped? Do you flip to the solution page and call it a day? If you were working a crossword puzzle, maybe you'd get some relief by doing so. ("Ahh . . . Precambrian. Of course.") But when you're working on a logic puzzle, you don't get much satisfaction from just seeing the completed grid. If you're not the one to figure out the solution, you're left feeling incomplete.

My advice? Don't give up. Don't keep yourself awake all night stressing over solutions, but don't give up either. Let the puzzle stew for a while, and come back to it when your brain is fresh. And if that doesn't work, what else can you do? Here are just a few ideas:

- ✔ **Remind yourself that the math is basic.** Rarely will you encounter a target number that can stump you for too long.

- ✔ **Focus on the cages with the fewest possible solutions.** When you get to the trickier puzzles, *fewest* may not mean two or three. But if you're comparing a cage with five possible solutions to a cage with four, focus on the one with four.

- ✔ **Ask yourself, "What if?"** Sometimes, when you have two or more candidates for a box (or two or more combinations of candidates for a cage), you can make some logical deductions by asking yourself what it would mean if a particular one of those options were the correct one. The logic of the puzzle enables you to see what other boxes (or cages) could be solved if that particular option were right — if the result of assuming that option is correct is an impossibility (a particular number occurring twice in a row or column, for example), you know the option that was the subject of your "What if?" question is wrong. At that point, you can experiment in the same way with a different option.

- ✔ **Work on more than one puzzle at a time.** Ease your frustration by working on a slightly less treacherous puzzle. After you regain your confidence by completing a different grid, take another stab at the one causing you so much grief.

Above all, remember that puzzles are fun — even when you start to suspect they're not.

Tapping Some Additional Resources

In the Introduction to this book, I explain that KenKen is fairly new to the Western world; it was launched in the United States in 2008. But the demand for KenKen puzzles was immediate and strong, and the result is that you can find the puzzles (along with a plethora of tips for solving them) in many print and online resources, including the ones I mention in this section.

If you subscribe to *The New York Times*, you can find KenKen puzzles in the print version, as well as at www.nytimes.com. Online, the publication posts six new puzzles daily.

The KenKen Web site

The place to look for all-inclusive information about KenKen is the Web site www.kenken.com. All KenKen puzzles are licensed by Nextoy, LLC, a toy and game company based in New York State. Nextoy owns and operates this Web site, which features everything from KenKen's history to a short video tutorial. You can even download a KenKen app to your smartphone. Plus, you can play KenKen to your heart's content — what fun! Just choose a grid size (from 4 × 4 to 9 × 9), and either solve the puzzle online or print out the grid and do it on paper.

The video tutorial on www.kenken.com covers the rules that I explain in this chapter and demonstrates how to work a fairly easy grid. The vast majority of people working KenKen puzzles can get along just fine with this basic level of information.

However, if you find yourself crossing over to the land of KenKen experts after tackling a good number of truly tough puzzles, check out the KenKen Web site for a tutorial written by International Chess Master, world-renowned artificial intelligence expert, and all-around brilliant person David Levy. Look for the Tutorial link under the How to Play tab; then click on the link that says "KenKen Tutorial, Harder Puzzles." In it, Levy walks you through the steps involved in working one of the most difficult 6 × 6 grid puzzles ever published.

Resources for teachers

As I note in the Introduction, I developed KenKen for use in my classroom in Japan. I wanted a tool to help students experience the true joys of learning and to improve their powers of logic.

KenKen is quickly making its way into U.S. classrooms, as well. The puzzle rules are simple enough for elementary students to learn, and the puzzles themselves can be challenging enough to keep students at every level engaged. If you're a teacher, you can sign up for the KenKen classroom program in order to receive KenKen puzzles for your students on a regular basis. Check out `kenken.com/signup/teacher.php` for details.

As more Western educators become familiar with the puzzle format, you'll undoubtedly be reading and hearing a lot more about KenKen and its many uses (and successes) in the classroom. KenKen is a lot of fun and a great way to get kids to enjoy expanding their math skills and logical thought processes. Feel free to start spreading the word now that you're on your way to becoming a KenKen aficionado!

Part II
KenKen Puzzlemania

The 5th Wave

By Rich Tennant

"It's a game of lining up numbers mathematically in such a way that you win. So how is it not like filling out your income tax?"

In this part . . .

If you haven't worked on KenKen puzzles before, get ready to become addicted! If you have, you already know how much fun you're going to have flipping through this part.

Here, you find an array of puzzles arranged in order of difficulty from easiest to most difficult. I strongly suggest that you don't dive into the baddest of the bad until you have some experience working with the easier grids. The goal here is to enjoy yourself and challenge your logic — not to destroy your self-esteem!

Chapter 2
Puzzles

Puzzle 1
Difficulty Level: Easy

+ −

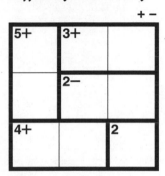

Puzzle 2
Difficulty Level: Easy

+ ×

3+	5+	1
		6×
4+		

Puzzle 3
Difficulty Level: Easy

+ ÷

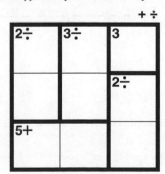

Puzzle 4
Difficulty Level: Easy

+ − ÷

5+	2÷	
	2−	
2÷		3

Puzzle 5
Difficulty Level: Easy

+ − × ÷

2×		11+	
	6×		
10+		2	2÷
	3−		

Puzzle 6
Difficulty Level: Easy

+ − × ÷

2÷		1	36×
3−	5+		
		4×	
3	3−		

Puzzle 7
Difficulty Level: Easy

+ − × ÷

7+	2÷	3−	
		2	6×
3−		7+	
6×			1

Puzzle 8
Difficulty Level: Easy

+ − × ÷

4	6×	4+	
3+		2	7+
	3−		
2−		2÷	

Puzzle 9
Difficulty Level: Easy

+ − × ÷

6×		5+	2÷
3−	3		
	3−	6×	7+
2			

Puzzle 10
Difficulty Level: Easy

+ − × ÷

3−		6×	3
7+			3+
	2	11+	
2÷			

Puzzle 11
Difficulty Level: Easy

+ − × ÷

2−		2−	
3−	6×	2÷	
		3	7+
2	3−		

Puzzle 12
Difficulty Level: Easy

+ − × ÷

6×	3	3−	
	2÷		1
2÷		7+	
3−		5+	

Puzzle 13
Difficulty Level: Easy

+ − × ÷

6×		4	3−
1	5+		
12×	2÷		5+
	3−		

Puzzle 14
Difficulty Level: Easy

+ − × ÷

5+		2÷	6×
3+	3		
	2÷	4+	
3		3−	

Puzzle 15
Difficulty Level: Easy

+ − × ÷

24×			3×
7+	4×		
			4
2−		2÷	

Puzzle 16
Difficulty Level: Easy

+ − × ÷

6×	3−	4+	
		32×	
3−	1−	2÷	
			3

Puzzle 17
Difficulty Level: Easy

+ − × ÷

7+	6×	3−	
		2÷	
1−		18×	4
3−			

Puzzle 18
Difficulty Level: Easy

+ − × ÷

1	2÷		9×
9+	2		
	3−		2÷
	4+		

Puzzle 19
Difficulty Level: Easy

+ − × ÷

2÷	12×		3−
	5+		
3	3−		5+
3−		2	

Puzzle 20
Difficulty Level: Easy

+ − × ÷

4	2÷		36×
2÷			
2−		2÷	
7+		2÷	

Puzzle 21
Difficulty Level: Easy

+ − × ÷

4+	7+	2−	
		3−	6×
2−	2÷		
		4+	

Puzzle 22
Difficulty Level: Easy

+ − × ÷

7+		3−	2÷
3+	18×		
			24×
5+			

Puzzle 23
Difficulty Level: Easy

+ − × ÷

6×	3−	2	4+
		7+	
3+			4
1−		2÷	

Puzzle 24
Difficulty Level: Easy

+ − × ÷

3−	3+	7+	3
			2÷
6×		1	
7+		1−	

Puzzle 25
Difficulty Level: Easy

+ − × ÷

3	2−	2÷	
3−		2÷	
	6×		4
2÷		4+	

Puzzle 26
Difficulty Level: Easy

+ − × ÷

2÷	1	12×	
	7+	1−	2
3			3−
2÷		3	

Puzzle 27
Difficulty Level: Easy

+ − × ÷

7+		2÷	
12×		3−	
	1	7+	6×
3−			

Puzzle 28
Difficulty Level: Easy

+ − × ÷

1−	3	3−	
	3−		3+
3−	2÷	6×	
			3

Puzzle 29
Difficulty Level: Easy

+ − × ÷

3−	16×		3
	10+		2÷
		12×	
2÷			

Puzzle 30
Difficulty Level: Easy

+ − × ÷

1	1−	3+	2−
7+			
	6×		4+
2÷		4	

Puzzle 31
Difficulty Level: Easy

+ − × ÷

3−	3+		6×
	7+		
5+	2÷	3−	
		2−	

Puzzle 32
Difficulty Level: Easy

+ − × ÷

3−		6×	
7+	7+		3−
		3−	
2÷			3

Puzzle 33
Difficulty Level: Easy

+ − × ÷

3+	12×	6×	
		2÷	4+
3−			
1−		3−	

Puzzle 34
Difficulty Level: Easy

+ − × ÷

4+	2	8×	24×
2÷	9×		
		3−	

Puzzle 35
Difficulty Level: Easy

+ − × ÷

2	3−		6×
7+	1−		
	1	48×	
2÷			

Puzzle 36
Difficulty Level: Easy

+ − × ÷

3+	3	2÷	
	3−	12×	
24×		2÷	4+

Puzzle 37
Difficulty Level: Easy

+ − × ÷

9×		3+	4
	3−		9+
2÷			
	6+		

Puzzle 38
Difficulty Level: Easy

+ − × ÷

3−		1−	
2÷	2	12×	
	7+		2÷
3	3−		

Puzzle 39
Difficulty Level: Easy

+ − × ÷

4+		3−	2÷
2÷	7+		
		6×	3
2÷			

Puzzle 40
Difficulty Level: Easy

+ − × ÷

1−	2−	2÷	
		4	2÷
3−	12×		
	3+		3

Puzzle 41
Difficulty Level: Easy

+ − × ÷

3+		4	12×
3	2÷		
2÷	7+		1−
	2−		

Puzzle 42
Difficulty Level: Easy

+ − × ÷

2÷	2−		4
	1−	2÷	
12×		2	4+
	3+		

Puzzle 43
Difficulty Level: Easy

+ − × ÷

4	9×	3+	2÷
2−		2−	
2÷		1−	

Puzzle 44
Difficulty Level: Easy

+ − × ÷

2÷	4+		3+
	1−	3−	
4+			12×
	2÷		

Puzzle 45
Difficulty Level: Easy

+ − × ÷

2÷		2−	
4+	3+		2÷
	4+	24×	
4			

Puzzle 46
Difficulty Level: Easy

+ − × ÷

3−	7+	1−	
		2÷	
6×		7+	5+
3+			

Puzzle 47
Difficulty Level: Easy

+ − × ÷

5+	2÷		9×
	2÷		
8+		2÷	
		3−	

Puzzle 48
Difficulty Level: Easy

+ − × ÷

1	3−	12×	
9+			3
	7+		3−
	2÷		

Puzzle 49
Difficulty Level: Easy

+ − × ÷

2÷	4+	6×	
		1−	3−
2−	2÷		
		12×	

Puzzle 50
Difficulty Level: Easy

+ − × ÷

12×	4+		2÷
	2÷		
2÷		7+	
3−		1−	

Puzzle 51
Difficulty Level: Easy

+ − × ÷

2÷	7+	6×	
		3−	
3×			2÷
	1−		

Puzzle 52
Difficulty Level: Easy

+ − × ÷

12×	1−		2÷
	3−		
	2	12×	4+
3+			

Puzzle 53
Difficulty Level: Easy

+ − × ÷

6×		2÷	
	7+	2−	
3−		24×	1
	2		

Puzzle 54
Difficulty Level: Easy

+ − × ÷

1	7+		1−
7+	1	2÷	
	12×		5+
		1	

Puzzle 55
Difficulty Level: Easy

+ − × ÷

3−		3	6×
2÷			
2−	9+		3−
	2		

Puzzle 56
Difficulty Level: Easy

+ − × ÷

7+	2÷	3−	
		2−	2÷
6×			
3−		1−	

Puzzle 57
Difficulty Level: Easy

+ − × ÷

2÷	6×		
	11+		2÷
2−		9+	
	1		

Puzzle 58
Difficulty Level: Easy

+ − × ÷

2−	2	16×	
	1−		
3−		4+	1−
2÷			

Puzzle 59
Difficulty Level: Easy

+ − × ÷

12×		2÷	
3	3+	2−	1−
1−			
	7+		1

Puzzle 60
Difficulty Level: Easy

+ − × ÷

2÷	2−		5+
	24×		
4+		2	5+
	5+		

Puzzle 61
Difficulty Level: Easy

+ − × ÷

4+		3−	1−
3+	12×		
		1−	3−
2÷			

Puzzle 62
Difficulty Level: Easy

+ − × ÷

2÷		3−	12×
5+			
1−	3−	2÷	
		5+	

Puzzle 63
Difficulty Level: Easy

+ − × ÷

3−	2÷	24×	
		10+	
9+			2÷
		1	

Puzzle 64
Difficulty Level: Easy

+ − × ÷

7+	6×	16×	
		3−	
2÷			2−
	1−		

Puzzle 65
Difficulty Level: Easy

+ − × ÷

3−		1−		12×
3+	5+	30×		
		5		
12×	9+		2÷	
	4+		3−	

Puzzle 66
Difficulty Level: Easy

+ − × ÷

18×	2÷		4−	
		4−	4	6×
9+				
1	20×	1−	2÷	
			2−	

Puzzle 67
Difficulty Level: Easy

+ − × ÷

1−	9+	12×		
		10×		5
5+	18×		2÷	
			9+	1−
5	3+			

Puzzle 68
Difficulty Level: Easy

+ − × ÷

5×		7+		9+
1−		3		
	3−		4−	6+
30×	2÷			
		9+		

Puzzle 69
Difficulty Level: Easy

+ − × ÷

9+	2−	2÷	2÷	
			2−	
2÷		60×		4−
12×			2	
3−		3	3−	

Puzzle 70
Difficulty Level: Easy

+ − × ÷

1−	2÷	9+		4−
		18×		
1−			4−	4
9+				1−
4−		2÷		

Puzzle 71
Difficulty Level: Easy

+ − × ÷

6×		4−		1−
	6×		9+	
12×	2÷			3
	9+		12×	
1−		1		

Puzzle 72
Difficulty Level: Easy

+ − × ÷

12×		4−	2÷	
3	11+		2÷	
4−			2−	
	1−		4−	7+
2÷		4		

Puzzle 73
Difficulty Level: Easy

+ − × ÷

3−	2−	3−	3+	4
				15×
2−	4	5+		
	4−		2÷	
9+			4−	

Puzzle 74
Difficulty Level: Easy

+ − × ÷

3−	2÷		1	180×
	4−			
1−		7+		
	90×		1−	2÷
1				

Puzzle 75
Difficulty Level: Easy

+ − × ÷

12×		9+	2÷	
	10×		4−	7+
2−		3+		
	8×		72×	
				5

Puzzle 76
Difficulty Level: Easy

+ − × ÷

3−	12×			4−
	7+		6×	
15×		7+		4
3−	2÷			1−
		4−		

Puzzle 77
Difficulty Level: Easy

+ − × ÷

2−	60×			2
	12×	3+	2	15×
2÷			20×	
	2÷	2−		
5			5+	

Puzzle 78
Difficulty Level: Easy

+ − × ÷

1−	2÷	1	12×	
		1−		4−
7+	9+		2	
		7+	4−	2÷
7+				

Puzzle 79
Difficulty Level: Easy

+ − × ÷

2÷	4−		12×	
	1−	3	9+	
1−		3−		3
	7+	2−	6+	2÷
5				

Puzzle 80
Difficulty Level: Easy

+ − × ÷

80×		3	1−	3+
1−		9+		
	2÷		8+	
2−		3−		1−
	6×		1	

Puzzle 81
Difficulty Level: Easy

+ − × ÷

1−		12×		9+
7+			2÷	
5+		11+		18×
20×				
	3		4−	

Puzzle 82
Difficulty Level: Easy

+ − × ÷

3	3+		20×	
2÷	180×			
	5	10×		1−
4−	2÷			
		12×		

Puzzle 83
Difficulty Level: Easy

+ − × ÷

1−	2÷		20×	
	2−		12+	4−
2÷		4		
13+		4+		
	5		2÷	

Puzzle 84
Difficulty Level: Easy

+ − × ÷

4−		3	120×	
9+	2÷			
	12×	4−	6×	
6×				10+
	2÷			

Puzzle 85
Difficulty Level: Easy

+ − × ÷

24×			15×	
2÷	4−		3+	
	2−	12×		3−
50×			11+	

Puzzle 86
Difficulty Level: Easy

+ − × ÷

4−		2÷		8+
3−	2÷	45×		
		4−		
11+			20×	
		4		

Puzzle 87
Difficulty Level: Easy

+ − × ÷

2÷		4−	13+	4
2÷	12×			4−
4−		96×		
2−			1−	

Puzzle 88
Difficulty Level: Easy

+ − × ÷

18×	1−		4−	
		3−	2÷	
	1		2−	3−
1−	2÷			
	4−		5+	

Puzzle 89
Difficulty Level: Easy

+ − × ÷

3−	3+		36×	60×
	11+			
1				
60×			2÷	
2−		2÷		5

Puzzle 90
Difficulty Level: Easy

+ − × ÷

4	3+		75×	
3+	5+	4−	48×	
15×	13+		1	2÷
		5+		

Puzzle 91
Difficulty Level: Easy

+ − × ÷

24×			4−	
1	2−		2÷	
2÷		9+		12×
3−		9×		
20×			2÷	

Puzzle 92
Difficulty Level: Tricky

+ − × ÷

1−		6×	1−	
4−	9+			20×
			4−	
3	2÷			4+
2÷		9+		

Puzzle 93
Difficulty Level: Tricky

+ − × ÷

2−		2−	2÷	3−
4−	12+			
		2÷	3−	
16×			2−	
		1	8+	

Puzzle 94
Difficulty Level: Tricky

+ − × ÷

2÷		20×		5+
12+	4−		5+	
	1−	3−		3−
			10+	
5+		3		

Puzzle 95
Difficulty Level: Tricky

+ − × ÷

2−		6×	15+	
2			15×	
20×				
60×		3−		3×
	2÷			

Puzzle 96
Difficulty Level: Tricky

+ − × ÷

2÷		9+		30×
4−	2÷		1−	
	1−	4−		
3			2÷	3−
12+				

Puzzle 97
Difficulty Level: Tricky

+ − × ÷

4	4−		6×	
8+			4−	2÷
8+	1−			
	7+		1−	4−
7+				

Puzzle 98
Difficulty Level: Tricky

+ − × ÷

1−	12×			4−
	12+	2÷		
		12+	4−	3
5+	2−			16×

Puzzle 99
Difficulty Level: Tricky

+ − × ÷

2÷		75×		2−
8+	5+			
	2÷		4+	
12+			10×	
2−		2−		

Puzzle 100
Difficulty Level: Tricky

+ − × ÷

4−	1−		2÷	5
	6×			5+
2÷	6+		15×	
	2	3−		1−
2−				

Puzzle 101
Difficulty Level: Tricky

+ − × ÷

60×		6+		1
		8+		10+
2÷			12×	
4−	6×			
		3	9+	

Puzzle 102
Difficulty Level: Tricky

+ − × ÷

12×			3−	
2÷		6×	6+	
2−			2÷	4+
	20×			
3+		12+		

Puzzle 103
Difficulty Level: Tricky

+ − × ÷

4−		20×	2÷	1−
2÷	5+			
			7+	7+
60×	1	1−		
			4−	

Puzzle 104
Difficulty Level: Tricky

+ − × ÷

2−		12×	3−	3−
2	2÷			
3−		6+		2−
	3	2÷		
20×			1−	

Puzzle 105
Difficulty Level: Tricky

+ − × ÷

8×	12+			1
	2	4−		2−
	5+	1−		
3		5+	3−	2÷
2−				

Puzzle 106
Difficulty Level: Tricky

+ − × ÷

3+	4−		12×	1−
	1−			
20×		2÷		6+
1−		20×		
	3	3−		

Puzzle 107
Difficulty Level: Tricky

+ − × ÷

6+		120×		
	4−			40×
60×		2÷		
	20×		7+	
2		3−		

Puzzle 108
Difficulty Level: Tricky

+ − × ÷

2÷		25×	7+	1−
3				
1−	4+	1−		5
		1−	2÷	
2÷			2−	

Puzzle 109
Difficulty Level: Tricky

+ − × ÷

9+	6×	2÷		6+
		11+		
3−			9+	
2−	5+	3−		24×

Puzzle 110
Difficulty Level: Tricky

+ − × ÷

12+			2÷	
2÷		6×	4−	1−
9+				
	4−		2÷	
	2−		8+	

Puzzle 111
Difficulty Level: Tricky

+ − × ÷

2−	2−	2÷		10×
		1	20×	
9+	1−	1−		1−
			3×	
11+				

Puzzle 112
Difficulty Level: Tricky

+ − × ÷

6+	4−	12×		
		1−		30×
	2÷			
1−	8+	2	4+	
			7+	

Puzzle 113
Difficulty Level: Tricky

+ − × ÷

4−	3	3+		24×
	1−			
2−		40×		
2÷	2−		1−	4−
	2÷			

Puzzle 114
Difficulty Level: Tricky

+ − × ÷

4−	2	12×		
	2−		1−	5+
2÷	4−	1−		
			200×	
1−		1		

Puzzle 115
Difficulty Level: Tricky

+ − × ÷

60×		6+		30×
2			12×	
4−	1−	2÷		
				5+
1−		5+		

Puzzle 116
Difficulty Level: Tricky

+ − × ÷

2÷		15×		
8+			3−	1−
1−	2÷			
	9+		3−	6×
20×				

Puzzle 117
Difficulty Level: Tricky

+ − × ÷

2−		2÷		15+
8×	1−			
	3−	3−		
		3−	4+	3−
2−				

Puzzle 118
Difficulty Level: Tricky

+ − × ÷

9+		15×		5+
3		10+		
4−			2−	
	12×	10+	2÷	
				5

Puzzle 119
Difficulty Level: Tricky

+ − × ÷

20×			5+	
1−		20×		
40×	3−		2−	
	15×	2÷		2÷
		2−		

Puzzle 120
Difficulty Level: Tricky

+ − × ÷

1−	8×		6+	
	5		2÷	7+
20×	2−			
	1−		8+	
	6+			

Puzzle 121
Difficulty Level: Tricky

+ − × ÷

4−		1−		12×
2÷	1−	9+		
				10+
7+	11+			
	6+			

Puzzle 122
Difficulty Level: Tricky

+ − × ÷

1−		10×	2−	
2−			9+	
2÷		6+	1−	
15×				5
		8×		

Puzzle 123
Difficulty Level: Tricky

+ − × ÷

3−	1−	2÷	15×	
			1−	
10+	1−		2÷	
	20×	40×		2−

Puzzle 124
Difficulty Level: Tricky

+ − × ÷

48×		4−	3−	
			6+	
2	4−	1−		
10+		2÷	12×	
			4−	

Puzzle 125
Difficulty Level: Easy

+ − × ÷

10×		2−		3÷	
5−	12×		3+		3−
	2÷	3−	10×	2−	
12×					5−
	8+	5	36×	96×	

Puzzle 126
Difficulty Level: Easy

+ − × ÷

3+		40×	2÷	24×	
3÷				15×	11+
	1−	5−	7+		
2−				5+	6×
	10+		5+		
30×				2÷	

Puzzle 127
Difficulty Level: Easy

+ − × ÷

2÷	2−		6+		45×
	3−	11+			
11+			5+	5−	
	1−	11+			2÷
2−			5	32×	
	4−				6

Puzzle 128
Difficulty Level: Easy

+ − × ÷

11+	13+	3+		15×	
			2÷		
2÷	5	18×			7+
	2÷	4−		3÷	
2−		15+	7+		3÷
				5	

Puzzle 129
Difficulty Level: Easy

+ − × ÷

11+		2−	120×	5+	
30×					3÷
2÷		15×		19+	
	3−		6×		
3		5−		10+	
24×					

Puzzle 130
Difficulty Level: Easy

+ − × ÷

5−	1−		3÷		10×
	3÷		9+		
3−		5		3−	
40×	1−		5−		72×
	3÷		3−		
	3−		11+		

Puzzle 131
Difficulty Level: Easy

+ − × ÷

60×		18×		60×	
3+			1		60×
	48×				
15×	24×			5−	
		100×	48×		
3÷				3÷	

Puzzle 132
Difficulty Level: Easy

+ − × ÷

6×	5−	24×	15×	2÷	
					30×
	1−	60×			
11+		10+			6×
	80×	2÷	3÷	10+	

Puzzle 133
Difficulty Level: Easy

+ − × ÷

12×	2÷		7+		5−
	1	2÷	15+		
6×				4−	
3−		5−		1−	
5−	1−	2÷		2÷	2÷
		15×			

Puzzle 134
Difficulty Level: Easy

+ − × ÷

20×	3÷	5+	5−	2−	4
					3÷
	1−		4−		
12×		5−	8+	240×	
2					
14+			7+		

Puzzle 135
Difficulty Level: Easy

+ − × ÷

10×			3÷	1−	3÷
8+	2÷	10+			
			5−		60×
2÷	5−	2−	3−		
			2÷	30×	
18×					

Puzzle 136
Difficulty Level: Easy

+ − × ÷

2−		3−		3×	
3+	24×		15×		
	3−	3÷	2÷		2−
8+			2÷		
	5−		20×		13+
1−		2÷			

Puzzle 137
Difficulty Level: Easy

+ − × ÷

2÷	2−		8+	24×	
	5−	2÷		3−	
1−			20×		3÷
	360×		5−		
30×			20×	3÷	
				12×	

Puzzle 138
Difficulty Level: Easy

+ − × ÷

5−	12×	12×		10+	
			3−		1−
72×				3÷	
200×	3−		6×		12×
	11+				
		3÷		10+	

Puzzle 139
Difficulty Level: Easy

+ − × ÷

1−		2÷	11+	6+	
12×				5−	
11+		3−		7+	
5	120×	5−		10+	
2÷					24×
		5+		5	

Puzzle 140
Difficulty Level: Easy

+ − × ÷

3−		72×			5−
3÷	3	20×	40×		
				11+	1−
3÷	5−		4		
	2−		3+		1−
2−		6×			

Puzzle 141
Difficulty Level: Easy

+ − × ÷

3÷		11+		2÷	
8×		2÷	9+		6
	2÷		2−		2−
11+		2−	5−		
	5		1−		2÷
2÷		6+		4	

Puzzle 142
Difficulty Level: Easy

+ − × ÷

75×	9+			3	5+
		3+	2−		
1−			1−		3÷
5−		1−	8+		
96×			3+		15×
	1	60×			

Puzzle 143
Difficulty Level: Easy

+ − × ÷

2−		5−		2÷	
16×	9+		5−		9×
		3÷	2−		
1−				3−	
5−	3÷		2−		30×
	1−		7+		

Puzzle 144
Difficulty Level: Easy

+ − × ÷

4−	5−		2÷		1−
	1−		2÷		
3+		1−		120×	
3	3÷		5×		
2−	7+	10×	2−		5−
				2	

Puzzle 145
Difficulty Level: Easy

+ − × ÷

2−		1−	5−	5+	
5−	3÷			1−	10×
		9+	7+		
9+	3−			11+	18×
		3÷			
	11+		2÷		

Puzzle 146
Difficulty Level: Easy

+ − × ÷

3−	1−		1−		12×
	7+		5−		
7+		7+		5−	
3÷	5−		12×		10×
	2−	20×		2−	
5		2÷			

Puzzle 147
Difficulty Level: Easy

+ − × ÷

4−		1−	3	2−	
3÷	3÷		8×	1−	11+
		7+			
1−				5−	
3÷	3−		11+		7+
	5+		6+		

Puzzle 148
Difficulty Level: Easy

+ − × ÷

20×			15+		5−
13+					
	48×			3÷	20×
2−	2	4−			
	5−		10×		5+
8+			11+		

Puzzle 149
Difficulty Level: Easy

+ − × ÷

10×		2÷		2÷	
	5−		2−	9+	3÷
120×	1−				
	3−		3÷	3+	1−
	216×				
		4−		3÷	

Puzzle 150
Difficulty Level: Easy

+ − × ÷

60×			3	3÷	
8×	3÷		21+		5
		14+			3×
5−	5		120×		
3	11+		8×		

Puzzle 151
Difficulty Level: Easy

+ − × ÷

11+		2	6×		12×
3−		11+			
2÷	1−	54×		10×	
			80×	5−	
5+				10+	6+
3−		3+			

Puzzle 152
Difficulty Level: Tricky

+ − × ÷

3÷		6×	5−	1−	
13+				3÷	
	24×		2−		2
3+			90×		
2÷	3−	15+	2	3−	3÷

Puzzle 153
Difficulty Level: Tricky

+ − × ÷

1−	60×		5+		3÷
	15+			5	
		3−		3−	
8×		2÷		3−	
20×		5−		10+	
	4−		3÷		

Puzzle 154
Difficulty Level: Tricky

+ − × ÷

1	120×		2÷	36×	
8+					3−
12+			15×		
6+			2−		1−
6×		3−	1−	10×	
11+					

Puzzle 155
Difficulty Level: Tricky

+ − × ÷

6+		24×	10+	3÷	
2−				3÷	
10×	2÷			5−	2÷
		11+	1−		
3÷				9+	
2÷		5−		2−	

Puzzle 156
Difficulty Level: Tricky

+ − × ÷

3−	3	24×		12×	15×
	6×		6+		
5−	1−				2−
	3−			13+	
8+	3÷		4		5−
		2−			

Puzzle 157
Difficulty Level: Tricky

+ − × ÷

2−		40×		10+	
3÷				2−	
5−	9+			6+	5
	15+				
5+		14+		4−	
6+				9+	

Puzzle 158
Difficulty Level: Tricky

$+ - \times \div$

144×		1—	2—	1—	
12+				5	8×
		5—			
2÷	20×		5+		1—
	3÷		24×		
1—		30×		3—	

Puzzle 159
Difficulty Level: Tricky

+ − × ÷

3−		6×		1−	
8+		5−	3−	2÷	
1−	3÷			8+	2÷
		1−			
7+		3−	30×	5−	
2÷				1−	

Puzzle 160
Difficulty Level: Tricky

+ − × ÷

1−	20×	2÷	3−	4−	
				11+	1−
90×			5+		
8+					5−
5−	5+	2−	7+		
				7+	

Puzzle 161
Difficulty Level: Tricky

+ − × ÷

2÷		1−	1−	30×	
14+				5	6+
	5−	5+	3−		
75×			3−		
		1−	2÷	3−	
1−				2−	

Puzzle 162
Difficulty Level: Tricky

+ − × ÷

11+		6×	3÷	2−	
30×				11+	
	12×	2−		50×	
1−					2÷
	32×			18×	
		11+			

Puzzle 163
Difficulty Level: Tricky

+ − × ÷

1−	2−		3+		5−
	24×		3÷	4−	
2÷		4−			15×
1−			30×	1−	
5−	1−				2÷
	2÷		1−		

Puzzle 164
Difficulty Level: Tricky

+ − × ÷

6×	15+		3+		4−
		3−		4	
9+		2÷	11+	11+	
5−					3÷
	11+		7+		
3−				2−	

Puzzle 165
Difficulty Level: Tricky

+ − × ÷

2−		6×		4−	
2÷		5−		2−	
5+	1−		4−		2÷
		8+	2−	2÷	
30×	2				2÷
	2−		1−		

Puzzle 166
Difficulty Level: Tricky

+ − × ÷

40×		5−		24×	
15+		2−			6×
	2÷	3−		5−	
		7+			
4+		2−	3−	600×	
3					

Puzzle 167
Difficulty Level: Tricky

+ − × ÷

2−	3−		11+	2÷	3÷
	1−				
2÷		12×		1−	
2÷		4−		2÷	
4−	3+		2÷	2−	2−
	3−				

Puzzle 168
Difficulty Level: Tricky

+ − × ÷

72×	2÷		14+		
		1−	5−		
15×				2÷	
3+		3÷	2−	13+	
10×	4				14+
		5+			

Puzzle 169
Difficulty Level: Tricky

+ − × ÷

2÷	6+			40×	
	5	14+	5−		3÷
				3	
15+			12+		6+
3−				8+	
	120×				

Puzzle 170
Difficulty Level: Tricky

+ − × ÷

3÷		24×		2−	
2−				2÷	
2÷		1−	60×	5−	
5−	15+			3÷	13+
3	4−		2÷		

Puzzle 171
Difficulty Level: Tricky

+ − × ÷

15×		2−		24×	
	5−		13+		
5−	1−				3−
	1−		10+		
2÷	11+		36×		5−
	8+				

Puzzle 172
Difficulty Level: Tricky

+ − × ÷

30×			1−	13+	
4−	20+			2÷	
			48×		5−
2÷	3÷			4−	
		4−			30×
16+					

Puzzle 173
Difficulty Level: Tricky

+ − × ÷

30×	5−		1−		2÷
		2−	6+		
6+	3÷			10+	5+
		2−	10×		
14+				18×	3−
	2−				

Puzzle 174
Difficulty Level: Tricky

+ − × ÷

6×		6+		6×	7+
1−	1−	3÷	1−		
				1−	
4−	2−	1−	5−		14+
				9+	
5+		1−			

Puzzle 175
Difficulty Level: Tricky

+ − × ÷

6×	4−		2÷		10+
	2−		13+		
2÷					12×
20×		48×			
5+	5+			21+	
	5−				

Puzzle 176
Difficulty Level: Tricky

+ − × ÷

5−	20×			3	1−
	13+		12+		
6×	2÷			5−	1−
		17+	72×		
12+			2÷		6

Puzzle 177
Difficulty Level: Tricky

+ − × ÷

1−		60×	80×	3−	
3−					3+
	12+	2÷	1−	10+	
1	7+		2÷	1−	
20×				1−	

Puzzle 178
Difficulty Level: Tricky

+ − × ÷

48×		1−		8+	
	2÷	5−	1−	7+	
11+					2−
	24×		6×		
2÷	1−		20×		2−
	15+				

Puzzle 179
Difficulty Level: Tricky

+ − × ÷

72×	2÷	5−		2−	2−
		8+	48×		
					5
2÷	3	1−		48×	
	16+	2−	1−	9+	

Puzzle 180
Difficulty Level: Tricky

+ − × ÷

2÷	1−		3−		3−
	1−		30×		
2−	3	1−	6+		3−
	2−			4−	
2−		5−			3−
	5−		1−		

Puzzle 181
Difficulty Level: Tricky

+ − × ÷

1−	72×	5	2÷	2÷	2−
3+		13+		30×	
1−		30×		1−	
3÷	12×			24×	1−

Puzzle 182
Difficulty Level: Tricky

+ − × ÷

13+	3−	4−		2−	11+
		1	40×		
	14+				
1−				5−	
1−		2÷	3÷	2−	
3+				1−	

Puzzle 183
Difficulty Level: Tricky

+ − × ÷

75×		2−	2−		9+
2÷			5−		
	3÷	2÷		2−	
18+		1−			6+
		3÷	1−		
			4−		6

Puzzle 184
Difficulty Level: Tricky

+ − × ÷

1−		3÷	1−	12×	
5+					10+
2−	5−	13+			
				13+	
2−		1−	5−	1	
5+				2−	

Puzzle 185
Difficulty Level: Treacherous

+ − × ÷

2÷	75×	3−		48×	
			3+		
18×			24×		6+
48×			13+		
3−	9+				10+
		3÷			

Puzzle 186
Difficulty Level: Treacherous

+ − × ÷

18×		2÷	48×	2−	
12+					12×
		15+			
48×			18+	4	5−
	12×			9+	

Puzzle 187
Difficulty Level: Treacherous

+ − × ÷

108×		6+		48×	
2÷			1−		
	3÷		6	1−	
120×	4−		9+		
	20×		6+		2÷
		2÷			

Puzzle 188
Difficulty Level: Treacherous

+ − × ÷

15×	15+	3−	1−	6+	
				24×	
		1−	1−		4
12+	6+			360×	
		11+	5+		
				3÷	

Puzzle 189
Difficulty Level: Treacherous

+ − × ÷

2÷	5−		2−		12×
	1−	20+		2÷	
1−		3÷			12+
	48×				
16+			2×		11+

Puzzle 190
Difficulty Level: Treacherous

+ − × ÷

10×		2−		2−	
9+			48×		
2÷	7+		13+		9+
	5−			9+	
2		144×			
20×				3÷	

Puzzle 191
Difficulty Level: Treacherous

+ − × ÷

5−		2÷	7+	1−	
54×				12+	
	2÷		1−		
17+			108×		
	1−	2÷	5−		7+

Puzzle 192
Difficulty Level: Treacherous

+ − × ÷

3−		18×	7+	2÷	
2−					2÷
	5−		9+		
6	10+		15+		
3÷				3−	
2÷		2−		5−	

Puzzle 193
Difficulty Level: Treacherous

+ − × ÷

90×		5−		2÷	
	14+				5−
1	60×	180×		10×	
		3−			
2÷				3−	
3−		3÷		2−	

Puzzle 194
Difficulty Level: Treacherous

+ − × ÷

3÷	1−		3÷	600×	
	2÷				
9+		3÷	3÷		1−
30×			1−		
3÷	2−		1−	11+	
	3−				1

Puzzle 195
Difficulty Level: Treacherous

+ − × ÷

30×		3	5−	10+	
15+		3÷			9+
	6×		10×		
			1−		
2÷		9+	1−	1−	
1−				5−	

Puzzle 196
Difficulty Level: Treacherous

+ − × ÷

5−	2÷		2−		3−
	12×		15+		
16+				8+	
12×		6×			9+
		2−	3÷		
5+				1−	

Puzzle 197
Difficulty Level: Treacherous

+ − × ÷

144×	4−		24×		
		10+			11+
	2÷	2÷	5−	2−	
24+					2÷
		6+			
		12×			

Puzzle 198
Difficulty Level: Treacherous

+ − × ÷

2÷		15+			12×
360×			2÷		
	3÷			15×	
10+	2÷		1−	6+	
				24×	
4−		13+			

Puzzle 199
Difficulty Level: Treacherous

+ − × ÷

36×		1−	2÷	2−	
8+				2÷	4
		2÷			3−
14+		2÷		24×	
	24×	6×	2−		
				2÷	

Puzzle 200
Difficulty Level: Treacherous

+ − × ÷

3÷		15×		3−	
12+				120×	2−
15+					
	90×		7+		14+
		1	72×		
3−					

Puzzle 201
Difficulty Level: Treacherous

+ − × ÷

12×			16+		30×
3−		144×			
3÷			2÷	18+	
	11+				
2			2÷	2−	
15+					

Puzzle 202
Difficulty Level: Treacherous

+ − × ÷

2÷	5−		2÷	3−	4−
	24×				
4−		15+			7+
	3÷		3÷		
2÷	2−		3−		4−
	4−		2−		

Puzzle 203
Difficulty Level: Treacherous

+ − × ÷

6×		7+		7+	
2÷	3÷		1−		2−
	3−		5−		
2−		1−		3÷	
20×		3÷		72×	
	5+		6+		

Puzzle 204
Difficulty Level: Treacherous

+ − × ÷

24×			3	3—	
4—	2÷	2÷	2÷		2—
			2÷	5—	
2÷	4—	2—			2—
			90×		
10+				3—	

Puzzle 205
Difficulty Level: Treacherous

+ − × ÷

90×		48×	12+		
			2÷	6×	
3−	5−				12×
		12+	2÷	1−	
48×					180×

Puzzle 206
Difficulty Level: Treacherous

+ − × ÷					
20×		2÷		24×	3÷
	15+				
2÷	4−		2÷		1−
	3÷			10+	
16×	10+				3÷
		3−			

Puzzle 207
Difficulty Level: Easy

+ − × ÷

20×	6−	10×	3÷	13+	8+	
					5+	
3	24×	6−		9+		13+
3+		4−			13+	
		72×				25×
13+	11+	12×	21×	2÷		
					2÷	

Puzzle 208
Difficulty Level: Treacherous

+ − × ÷

2	15+	6×		1−	20+	
			3−			
168×	18+			8+		17+
	24×				2−	
		24×				
	6−		2÷	2÷		
15×				7	2÷	

Puzzle 209
Difficulty Level: Treacherous

+ − × ÷

2−		10×		24+		
3÷	1−	12+		21×		
					2÷	
6×		5	2−		10+	
3−	6×	126×	60×		4−	
					8×	
12+		1−		5−		

Puzzle 210
Difficulty Level: Treacherous

+ − × ÷

112×		12+	18×		3−	
			12+			
10+	20×		3	3528×		
	18+		2÷		1	
	9+					
18×	35×	11+	12+			
				2−		

Puzzle 211
Difficulty Level: Treacherous

+ − × ÷

210×			1−	12+		
20+	1−			196×	3÷	
		2÷				
	24+	12+			6+	1
		13+		24×		
		2÷	1−		2−	
				13+		

Puzzle 212
Difficulty Level: Treacherous

+ − × ÷

288×			23+		4−	
12×			3		19+	
			42×			
10×	12+			7+		3−
	8+	1−		3÷	1−	
1−			1−			1−
	1−			6−		

Puzzle 213
Difficulty Level: Treacherous

+ − × ÷

1−	28×		14+			5−
		2÷	5+	1−		
2÷	15×				3−	5−
		480×				
11+		6−			1−	
1−	12+	30×			2÷	1−
			2÷			

Puzzle 214
Difficulty Level: Treacherous

+ − × ÷

1−	2÷		42×			8+
	6−		1−	3÷		
2÷		13+		15+	1−	
5−			1			2÷
	8+		9+	10+		
1−		17+			3−	
4−					5+	

Puzzle 215
Difficulty Level: Treacherous

+ − × ÷

5−		3−		12×		15+
2÷	5−	13+	1−	4−		
				12+	6−	
4−		9+				6
15×	2−	8+			24×	
				5−		
10+		2÷		1−		

Puzzle 216
Difficulty Level: Treacherous

+ − × ÷

12+		24×			2−	
		13+	180×		1−	2−
210×	1−					
			1	17+		
	5		13+		5+	3÷
336×		30×				
		70×			5−	

Puzzle 217
Difficulty Level: Treacherous

+ − × ÷

84×		10+			10+	
6+		18+				14+
	18×		35×		168×	
10+		3−		3	6−	
140×		84×			12+	
	6+			2÷		

Puzzle 218
Difficulty Level: Treacherous

+ − × ÷

7	2−	2÷	70×	7+	12+	
2−						1−
	56×	2−		5−	13+	
			7+			
1−	1−			6−		12×
	6−		1−	9+		
2−		5			8+	

Puzzle 219
Difficulty Level: Treacherous

+ − × ÷

105×			2÷		13+	5+
6−	28×	7+	1−			
				10+		168×
7+		6	16+			
12×	5−				11+	
			9+			1−
48×			8+			

Puzzle 220
Difficulty Level: Treacherous

+ − × ÷

6+		72×			14×	
4−	2÷	10+		2−		2÷
			18+			
2÷		10×	5−		3−	
1−	1−		15×			2÷
			84×	15+		
1−					1−	

Puzzle 221
Difficulty Level: Treacherous

+ − × ÷

126×	11+		2÷		2÷	
			20+		3−	
13+				84×	4−	
1−		12×			90×	7
		14+				
12×				6+	14+	
	1−				5	

Puzzle 222
Difficulty Level: Treacherous

+ − × ÷

2−	21×		9+		1−	3−
		3−	2520×			
105×	8+				224×	1
						21×
	24×	1−				
2÷				15+	3÷	24×
	1−					

Puzzle 223
Difficulty Level: Treacherous

+ − × ÷

48×		9+	3−	42×	6×	6−
	5−					
10×			14+	2÷		14+
	3−			3−		
	3−	15+		1−		
126×			1−	4−	8+	2÷

Puzzle 224
Difficulty Level: Treacherous

+ − × ÷

6×	19+			3÷		3−
	8×		168×	8+		
				18+	8+	
42×		7+			1−	
420×		6+			4−	
11+		8+		3−		1−
				2−		

Puzzle 225
Difficulty Level: Treacherous

+ − × ÷

21×		14+			1−	
23+				1−	2÷	
		2−			9+	84×
4	3−		2÷			
15+		42×		6+		
	3−		8+		4−	
2−				14+		

Puzzle 226
Difficulty Level: Easy

+ − × ÷

18×		15+	10+	6−		120×	
36×					5−		
	200×	4−		3×		2−	7
			21×				7+
15+	3+	1	2÷		2÷		
		10×		24×		21×	
4	140×	2÷	5−	3÷	13+	7−	
						3÷	

Puzzle 227
Difficulty Level: Treacherous

+ − × ÷

24×		5−	7−	2−		2÷	
11+				6+	192×		12+
28×	2÷					3÷	
	210×			17+			2÷
5−		1−		12×		11+	
	3−		7				
2÷		3−		3−	20+		192×
6×		4−					

Puzzle 228
Difficulty Level: Treacherous

+ − × ÷

120×		56×		13+			3−
	21×				1−	2÷	
4−	7+		18+				2÷
		2÷			2÷		
40×	3÷		42×	2÷		2−	
		80×			120×	21×	
12×			1−			18+	
4÷				8+			

Puzzle 229
Difficulty Level: Treacherous

+ − × ÷

2−	10+	1−		4÷		100×	
		96×	2−	6−	1−		
15×						5−	
			4−		4−		42×
	21+	6+		1−	3−	8	
			14×			12+	
15+				3÷			7+
2−		5−		2−			

Puzzle 230
Difficulty Level: Treacherous

+ − × ÷

2÷	6−	5−	3−		2−	105×	
			2÷	14×			4÷
2−		12×				160×	
14×			4−	1			1−
	12+	1−		16+			
			42×			7+	
2−	4÷		6+		4−		3−
	1−		10+				

Puzzle 231
Difficulty Level: Treacherous

+ − × ÷

60×			18+		6−		7−
2÷		336×			1−	3÷	
3−	4÷						210×
	15+		15+	7−	12×		
5−	4÷					2÷	3−
		10+	3−	5−			
3−				6+	9+	3−	
	1−					2÷	

Puzzle 232
Difficulty Level: Treacherous

+ − × ÷

96×		40×	8+		2−	2−	
4÷				2		630×	
	2−	168×			15+		
280×		3−		2÷		2÷	
			19+		12+	6+	9+
2	20×	28×					
126×				1−		96×	7−
		1−					

Puzzle 233
Difficulty Level: Treacherous

+ − × ÷

126×			12+		5	56×	
20+	20×			19+			
		15+		6−		2÷	
	10×				48×		48×
4÷	5−	30×				2−	
		1−		80×	14×		13+
48×	15+						
		11+				2−	

Puzzle 234
Difficulty Level: Treacherous

+ − × ÷

12×	16+			30×			3÷
	21×	13+		8+	20+		
35×						4	3−
		2÷		3−	70×		
11+		192×				7+	
7−		18+		2−		3÷	3−
				80×	3÷		
3÷		4				4−	

Puzzle 235
Difficulty Level: Treacherous

+ − × ÷

28×		2−		8+	18+		30×
21+						6×	
7−	2÷	2÷	4−		21×		
			10+	4−		12+	
2÷		490×				16+	
1−				5−			
2÷	2−		14+			2÷	
		1	2÷		15+		

Puzzle 236
Difficulty Level: Treacherous

+ − × ÷

24×	13+		15+	1−		5−	
					24×		210×
3−		12×		16+			
16+			2÷			20×	
2−		4÷		2−	3÷		12+
	11+	180×					
6−			1−		4	7−	
		20+			36×		

Puzzle 237
Difficulty Level: Treacherous

+ − × ÷

224×			3÷	9+		24+	
13+	4−	2÷		6×		2−	
					5		
	30×	2−	11+		96×		3−
			15+			2÷	
2−	4−	192×		5−			6+
			3−		112×	4−	
7−		1−					

Puzzle 238
Difficulty Level: Treacherous

+ − × ÷

2	12×		20+			48×	
1−		8+		4÷	3÷	5−	1−
12+			4−				
	26+	4÷		3÷		3−	
4÷			2−	2−		1−	5
		15+		9+	11+		2÷
1−						12+	
	2÷		6	35×			

Puzzle 239
Difficulty Level: Treacherous

+ − × ÷

1−		56×		2−		21+	
16+	1−	1−	2÷		3÷		
			13+	24×		1	6−
	4				13+		
7−	1−	24×		40×		120×	
		7−	5−		140×	11+	
16+							2−
		6+		7			

Puzzle 240
Difficulty Level: Treacherous

+ − × ÷

10+	24×		12+	7−		2−	
		8+			2÷		7−
30×				9+	27+		
36×		5−					7
	2−		15+			1−	
		7	1−	2÷	10+	3÷	
19+	3−					3÷	
		4÷		1−		6×	

Puzzle 241
Difficulty Level: Treacherous

+ − × ÷

14×	60×	2÷		2−		1−	2−
			280×	7+			
6					10+		
7−		13+			7	3−	5−
3−		1−	30×		96×		
24×							
3÷	1−		7	2−		1−	
	26+				7+		

Puzzle 242
Difficulty Level: Treacherous

+ − × ÷

28×			2−	6	25+		17+
1−		24×					
6+	60×		8×	18+		2÷	
						1−	
16+	3÷		13+	1−	7−		8+
	4÷				13+		
	240×	19+		7−	13+		

Puzzle 243
Difficulty Level: Easy

+ − × ÷

4−	17+		6+	12×	13+		2	64×
	16+					5		
20×		8+	15+			8−	54×	5−
3+			224×					
3÷	252×			40×		5+		54×
	4	1−		8−		8+		
13+	3+		4÷	18×		3−		
	2÷			13+		8+		140×
15+		3÷		2	3−			

Puzzle 244
Difficulty Level: Treacherous

+ − × ÷

360×			252×	7−		3	1−	
	1−	40×		10+				90×
6×				5−		18+	14×	
	72×			2−	9+			
6×	8+		19+				168×	
	8−				2÷			4
2÷		63×	8+	4		60×	4−	2−
	3				22+			
1−		1−					4÷	

Puzzle 245
Difficulty Level: Treacherous

+ − × ÷

8−	6	70×			5−		17+	
	180×	2	12×	18+		2−		
					1−	9+		15+
18+			3÷			5−	16+	
42×		120×		2÷				
			13+		4−	64×		
	2−	1−	7−	12+			2−	
2−					1−			126×
	28×				2−			

Puzzle 246
Difficulty Level: Treacherous

+ − × ÷

2÷		35+					4−	108×
3÷	5−	224×	5−		4−			
			20×	3÷	108×			
3−	14+		14+					384×
		8−		1−		14+		
216×			1−				100×	
	2÷	6−		7+	36×			14×
17+		11+			7−		3÷	
		2−		2−		8		

Puzzle 247
Difficulty Level: Treacherous

+ − × ÷

42×	270×		12+	1	2÷	4−		144×
				5−		2÷		
	448×	8−			13+			
		18+	7+		18×		17+	
5			126×			8×		
24×		21+	32×	6+			504×	2−
7−		21+			105×	8−		1−
	8×					2−		

Puzzle 248
Difficulty Level: Treacherous

+ − × ÷

45×		10+			5−	2−		3−
16×		23+				8−		
			90×	1−		2−		16+
11+	19+			4÷		4÷		
				1−		30×		
21+		7	8−		180×			
42×		2−	252×	3−		1−	4−	6×
				210×				
108×						2÷		

Puzzle 249
Difficulty Level: Treacherous

+ − × ÷

3÷	12×		4−	1−	576×		2−	36×
	1−					9		
840×				3÷		4÷		
3−	7−	1−	7−	9+	2÷	240×		
						3÷		14+
5	2÷		18+			84×		
2÷		13+		280×		5−		
504×	36×		13+				4−	5−
		15+						

Puzzle 250
Difficulty Level: Treacherous

+ − × ÷

24+	1568×		9+		5	14+	1−	
			8−		12×		3÷	
	2÷			3456×			140×	
	3÷	18+			3÷			12+
18+						14×		
		15×		196×		2÷		2÷
280×		13+	210×		144×		29+	
								8
4÷				4−				

Puzzle 251
Difficulty Level: Treacherous

+ − × ÷

1−	2÷		20×	26+		1512×	2÷	
	4−							
18+	8−				42×		18+	
	1−	189×		10+	6−			
			5−		9	240×		
1−		60×			2÷		20+	
1260×				72×	8+			
		2−	9+			16+	4−	
3÷				3−				6

Puzzle 252
Difficulty Level: Treacherous

+ − × ÷

11+	280×		20+	160×	7−	1−	3−	2÷
48×	6×	30×			36×		2÷	35+
				11+				
13+	4−	13+		15+	17+	16+		
		3÷					8+	
	8−		1−					
4−		24×	1−	1−		224×		
					40×		4−	

Puzzle 253
Difficulty Level: Treacherous

+ − × ÷

504×	5−	120×		7−	8−		14+	
		3÷			3÷	2÷	14+	
	12+		5−					
		22+			14×	3÷	4÷	4−
360×			5−					
	12×		7−	64×		2−		10+
21×					3−		756×	
180×		7−		105×				
	2÷				2−		17+	

Puzzle 254
Difficulty Level: Treacherous

+ − × ÷

1−	2÷		60×		3÷		4−	
	1323×		5−		2÷	10+		
1−				2−		11+		
	45×	13+			3÷		24×	30+
18×			2÷		14+			
	11+		3÷		2−			
2×		20+				288×		
2÷				8−	4−		28×	
	8	2÷				18+		

Puzzle 255
Difficulty Level: Treacherous

+ − × ÷

3÷	2÷		3÷	2−	70×		4−	
	7+				15+		2	56×
5−		15+				5−	42×	
1−		126×		20+				
56×						8−		144×
		15+		3−	252×		5−	
144×	20×							
		10+		1−		144×		4−
5−			18+			6		

Puzzle 256
Difficulty Level: Treacherous

+ − × ÷

48×			96×		8−	10+	1−	3−
14+		3−		168×				
1134×			4−		13+		1−	
		5				128×		315×
28×			11+					
3−	6+		4÷	10+	3−		14+	
		16+			10+	1−		
17+			12+			2−	5−	7+
			90×					

Puzzle 257
Difficulty Level: Treacherous

+ − × ÷

63×		4÷	48×	360×			7+	
144×	3			8×		2−	6+	
		1−			14+		60×	2÷
2÷			2−					
	12+			13+	1−			7−
2÷		4−	14+		5−	6−		
6+						20+		
7+	24+		1−		24×		5−	14×
		15+						

Puzzle 258
Difficulty Level: Treacherous

+ − × ÷

12×		4−	2÷	1−		14+		14+
3−	1−			8−				
		5−		9	72×	2−	2÷	
23+	1−		70×				3÷	
	4÷					21+		3−
	5−		4−	9+				
11+	1−			5−		64×	648×	
	6	6−	19+		18+			
10+							2÷	

Puzzle 259
Difficulty Level: Treacherous

+ − × ÷

1−	3÷	1−		35×		2÷	30×	10+
		256×		23+				
11+						4−	2÷	
4−	256×	30+					16+	
		630×		8−	48×			
					96×		7	16+
10+	6	54×	1−		14+			
	10+		14+				6−	
		6+			3−		5−	

Part III

Satisfying Your Need to Be Right: Solutions

The 5th Wave   By Rich Tennant

"You taped the KenKen puzzles to the windshield because you thought it would be safer to keep both hands on the wheel while you drove and solved the puzzles. And this is a game that's supposed to enhance your powers of logic?"

In this part . . .

When you become adept at filling in the KenKen grid, you may not need to check the solutions. With this type of puzzle, you know when you've got it right — the results are crystal clear. But when you first start working through KenKen puzzles, you may find it reassuring to check your work and make certain you haven't misunderstood something.

Plus, let's get real: When you tackle the larger and tougher grids, you're bound to come across some that simply stump you. Although I encourage you not to jump to the solution page at the first hint of frustration, I do have a heart. I know what it's like when a puzzle gets under your skin and you can't rest until it's solved. So if you just can't hold out any longer, feel free to flip to the solution and find out where you went wrong. I promise no one will think less of you!

Chapter 3
Solutions

. . . .

Puzzle 1

+ −

5+	3+	
3	**2**	**1**
2	2− **1**	**3**
4+ **1**	**3**	2 **2**

Puzzle 2

+ ×

3+	5+	1
2	**3**	**1**
1	**2**	6× **3**
4+ **3**	**1**	**2**

Puzzle 3

+ ÷

2÷	3÷	3
2	**1**	**3**
1	**3**	2÷ **2**
5+ **3**	**2**	**1**

Puzzle 4

+ − ÷

5+	2÷	
3	**1**	**2**
2	2− **3**	**1**
2÷ **1**	**2**	3 **3**

Puzzle 5

+ − × ÷

2× 2	1	11+ 4	3
1	6× 2	3	4
10+ 4	3	2 2	2÷ 1
3	3− 4	1	2

Puzzle 6

+ − × ÷

2÷ 2	4	1 1	36× 3
3− 1	5+ 2	3	4
4	3	4× 2	1
3 3	3− 1	4	2

Puzzle 7

+ − × ÷

7+ 3	2÷ 2	3− 1	4
4	1	2 2	6× 3
3− 1	4	7+ 3	2
6× 2	3	4	1 1

Puzzle 8

+ − × ÷

4 4	6× 2	4+ 3	1
3+ 1	3	2 2	7+ 4
2	3− 4	1	3
2− 3	1	2÷ 4	2

Puzzle 9

+ − × ÷

6× 3	2	5+ 4	2÷ 1
3− 4	3 3	1	2
1	3− 4	6× 2	7+ 3
2 2	1	3	4

Puzzle 10

+ − × ÷

3− 1	4	6× 2	3 3
7+ 4	3	1	3+ 2
3	2 2	11+ 4	1
2÷ 2	1	3	4

Puzzle 11

+ − × ÷

2− 3	1	2− 4	2
3− 4	6× 3	2÷ 2	1
1	2	3 3	7+ 4
2 2	3− 4	1	3

Puzzle 12

+ − × ÷

6× 2	3 3	3− 1	4
3	2÷ 4	2	1 1
2÷ 1	2	7+ 4	3
3− 4	1	5+ 3	2

Puzzle 13

+ − × ÷

6× 2	3	4 4	3− 1
1 1	5+ 2	3	4
12× 4	2÷ 1	2	5+ 3
3	3− 4	1	2

Puzzle 14

+ − × ÷

5+ 4	1	2÷ 2	6× 3
3+ 1	3 3	4	2
2	2÷ 4	4+ 3	1
3 3	2	3− 1	4

Puzzle 15

+ − × ÷

24× 2	4	3	3× 1
7+ 4	4× 2	1	3
3	1	2	4 4
2− 1	3	2÷ 4	2

Puzzle 16

+ − × ÷

6× 2	3− 4	4+ 3	1
3	1	32× 4	2
3− 1	1− 3	2÷ 2	4
4	2	1	3 3

Puzzle 17

+ − × ÷

7+ 3	6× 2	3− 4	1
4	3	2÷ 1	2
1− 2	1	18× 3	4 4
3− 1	4	2	3

Puzzle 18

+ − × ÷

1 1	2÷ 4	2	9× 3
9+ 4	2 2	3	1
3	3− 1	4	2÷ 2
2	4+ 3	1	4

Puzzle 19

+ − × ÷

2÷ 2	12× 3	4	3− 1
1	5+ 2	3	4
3 3	3− 4	1	5+ 2
3− 4	1	2 2	3

Puzzle 20

+ − × ÷

4 4	2÷ 2	1	36× 3
2÷ 2	1	3	4
2− 1	3	2÷ 4	2
7+ 3	4	2÷ 2	1

Puzzle 21

+ − × ÷

4+ 1	7+ 3	2− 2	4
3	4	3− 1	6× 2
2− 2	2÷ 1	4	3
4	2	4+ 3	1

Puzzle 22

+ − × ÷

7+ 3	4	3− 1	2÷ 2
3+ 2	18× 3	4	1
1	2	3	24× 4
5+ 4	1	2	3

Puzzle 23

+ − × ÷

6×	3−	2	4+
3	**4**	**2**	**1**
2	**1**	**4** 7+	**3**
3+ **1**	**2**	**3**	4 **4**
1− **4**	**3**	2÷ **1**	**2**

Puzzle 24

+ − × ÷

3−	3+	7+	3
1	**2**	**4**	**3**
4	**1**	**3**	2÷ **2**
6× **2**	**3**	1 **1**	**4**
7+ **3**	**4**	1− **2**	**1**

Puzzle 25

+ − × ÷

3	2−	2÷	
3	**1**	**4**	**2**
3− **4**	**3**	2÷ **2**	**1**
1	6× **2**	**3**	4 **4**
2÷ **2**	**4**	4+ **1**	**3**

Puzzle 26

+ − × ÷

2÷	1	12×	
2	**1**	**4**	**3**
4	7+ **3**	1− **1**	2 **2**
3 **3**	**4**	**2**	3− **1**
2÷ **1**	**2**	3 **3**	**4**

Puzzle 27

+ − × ÷

7+		2÷	
4	**3**	**2**	**1**
12× **3**	**2**	3− **1**	**4**
2	1 **1**	7+ **4**	6× **3**
3− **1**	**4**	**3**	**2**

Puzzle 28

+ − × ÷

1−	3	3−	
2	**3**	**1**	**4**
3	3− **1**	**4**	3+ **2**
3− **4**	2÷ **2**	6× **3**	**1**
1	**4**	**2**	3 **3**

Puzzle 29

+ − × ÷

3− **1**	16× **2**	**4**	3 **3**
4	10+ **3**	**2**	2÷ **1**
3	**4**	12× **1**	**2**
2÷ **2**	**1**	**3**	**4**

Puzzle 30

+ − × ÷

1 **1**	1− **3**	3+ **2**	2− **4**
7+ **3**	**4**	**1**	**2**
4	6× **2**	**3**	4+ **1**
2÷ **2**	**1**	4 **4**	**3**

Puzzle 31

+ − × ÷

3− **4**	3+ **1**	**2**	6× **3**
1	7+ **3**	**4**	**2**
5+ **3**	2÷ **2**	3− **1**	**4**
2	**4**	2− **3**	**1**

Puzzle 32

+ − × ÷

3− **1**	**4**	6× **3**	**2**
7+ **4**	7+ **3**	**2**	3− **1**
3	**2**	3− **1**	**4**
2÷ **2**	**1**	**4**	3 **3**

Puzzle 33

+ − × ÷

3+ **1**	12× **4**	6× **3**	**2**
2	**3**	2÷ **4**	4+ **1**
3− **4**	**1**	**2**	**3**
1− **3**	**2**	3− **1**	**4**

Puzzle 34

+ − × ÷

4+ **3**	2 **2**	8× **1**	24× **4**
1	**4**	**2**	**3**
2÷ **4**	9× **1**	**3**	**2**
2	**3**	3− **4**	**1**

Puzzle 35

+ − × ÷

2 **2**	3− **4**	**1**	6× **3**
7+ **4**	1− **3**	**2**	**1**
3	1 **1**	48× **4**	**2**
2÷ **1**	**2**	**3**	**4**

Puzzle 36

+ − × ÷

3+ **1**	3 **3**	2÷ **4**	**2**
2	3− **1**	12× **3**	**4**
24× **3**	**4**	2÷ **2**	4+ **1**
4	**2**	**1**	**3**

Puzzle 37

+ − × ÷

9× **1**	**3**	3+ **2**	4 **4**
3	3− **4**	**1**	9+ **2**
2÷ **2**	**1**	**4**	**3**
4	6+ **2**	**3**	**1**

Puzzle 38

+ − × ÷

3− **4**	**1**	1− **2**	**3**
2÷ **1**	2 **2**	12× **3**	**4**
2	7+ **3**	**4**	2÷ **1**
3 **3**	3− **4**	**1**	**2**

Puzzle 39

+ − × ÷

4+ **3**	**1**	3− **4**	2÷ **2**
2÷ **2**	7+ **3**	**1**	**4**
1	**4**	6× **2**	3 **3**
2÷ **4**	**2**	**3**	**1**

Puzzle 40

+ − × ÷

1− **3**	2− **1**	2÷ **2**	**4**
2	**3**	4 **4**	2÷ **1**
3− **1**	12× **4**	**3**	**2**
4	3+ **2**	**1**	3 **3**

Puzzle 41

$+ - \times \div$

3+		4	12×
1	**2**	**4**	**3**
3	2÷		
3	**1**	**2**	**4**
2÷	7+		1−
2	**4**	**3**	**1**
	2−		
4	**3**	**1**	**2**

Puzzle 42

$+ - \times \div$

2÷	2−		4
2	**1**	**3**	**4**
		1−	2÷
1	**3**	**4**	**2**
12×		2	4+
3	**4**	**2**	**1**
	3+		
4	**2**	**1**	**3**

Puzzle 43

$+ - \times \div$

4	9×	3+	2÷
4	**3**	**1**	**2**
3	**1**	**2**	**4**
2−		2−	
2	**4**	**3**	**1**
2÷		1−	
1	**2**	**4**	**3**

Puzzle 44

$+ - \times \div$

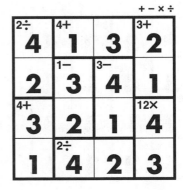

2÷	4+		3+
4	**1**	**3**	**2**
	1−	3−	
2	**3**	**4**	**1**
4+			12×
3	**2**	**1**	**4**
	2÷		
1	**4**	**2**	**3**

Puzzle 45

$+ - \times \div$

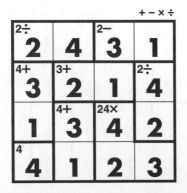

2÷		2−	
2	**4**	**3**	**1**
4+	3+		2÷
3	**2**	**1**	**4**
	4+	24×	
1	**3**	**4**	**2**
4			
4	**1**	**2**	**3**

Puzzle 46

$+ - \times \div$

3−	7+	1−	
1	**4**	**2**	**3**
		2÷	
4	**3**	**1**	**2**
6×		7+	5+
3	**2**	**4**	**1**
3+			
2	**1**	**3**	**4**

Puzzle 47

+ − × ÷

5+ 1	2÷ 4	2	9× 3
4	2÷ 2	3	1
8+ 3	1	2÷ 4	2
2	3	3− 1	4

Puzzle 48

+ − × ÷

1 1	3− 4	12× 3	2
9+ 4	1	2	3 3
2	7+ 3	4	3− 1
3	2÷ 2	1	4

Puzzle 49

+ − × ÷

2÷ 4	4+ 1	6× 3	2
2	3	1− 1	3− 4
2− 3	2÷ 4	2	1
1	2	12× 4	3

Puzzle 50

+ − × ÷

12× 4	4+ 3	1	2÷ 2
3	2÷ 2	4	1
2÷ 2	1	7+ 3	4
3− 1	4	1− 2	3

Puzzle 51

+ − × ÷

2÷ 4	7+ 3	6× 2	1
2	4	3− 1	3
3× 3	1	4	2÷ 2
1	1− 2	3	4

Puzzle 52

+ − × ÷

12× 1	1− 3	2	2÷ 4
3	3− 4	1	2
4	2 2	12× 3	4+ 1
3+ 2	1	4	3

Puzzle 53

+ − × ÷

6× 3	1	2÷ 4	2
2	7+ 4	2− 1	3
3− 4	3	24× 2	1 1
1	2 2	3	4

Puzzle 54

+ − × ÷

1 1	7+ 4	3	1− 2
7+ 4	1 1	2÷ 2	3
3	12× 2	4	5+ 1
2	3	1 1	4

Puzzle 55

+ − × ÷

3− 4	1	3 3	6× 2
2÷ 2	4	1	3
2− 1	9+ 3	2	3− 4
3	2 2	4	1

Puzzle 56

+ − × ÷

7+ 3	2÷ 2	3− 4	1
4	1	2− 3	2÷ 2
6× 2	3	1	4
3− 1	4	1− 2	3

Puzzle 57

+ − × ÷

2÷ 4	6× 2	1	3
2	11+ 3	4	2÷ 1
2− 1	4	9+ 3	2
3	1 1	2	4

Puzzle 58

+ − × ÷

2− 3	2 2	16× 4	1
1	1− 3	2	4
3− 4	1	4+ 3	1− 2
2÷ 2	4	1	3

Puzzle 59

12× 4	3	2÷ 1	2
3 3	3+ 1	2− 2	1− 4
1− 1	2	4	3
2	7+ 4	3	1 1

Puzzle 60

2÷ 2	2− 3	1	5+ 4
4	24× 2	3	1
4+ 1	4	2 2	5+ 3
3	5+ 1	4	2

Puzzle 61

4+ 3	1	3− 4	1− 2
3+ 2	12× 4	1	3
1	3	1− 2	3− 4
2÷ 4	2	3	1

Puzzle 62

2÷ 1	2	3− 4	12× 3
5+ 2	3	1	4
1− 3	3− 4	2÷ 2	1
4	1	5+ 3	2

Puzzle 63

3− 4	2÷ 1	24× 2	3
1	2	10+ 3	4
9+ 2	3	4	2÷ 1
3	4	1 1	2

Puzzle 64

7+ 3	6× 1	16× 2	4
4	3	3− 1	2
2÷ 1	2	4	2− 3
2	4	1− 3	1

Puzzle 65

+ − × ÷

3− **5**	**2**	1− **3**	**4**	12× **1**
3+ **1**	5+ **4**	30× **2**	**5**	**3**
2	**1**	5 **5**	**3**	**4**
12× **3**	9+ **5**	**4**	2÷ **1**	**2**
4	4+ **3**	**1**	3− **2**	**5**

Puzzle 66

+ − × ÷

18× **3**	2÷ **2**	**4**	4− **1**	**5**
2	**3**	4− **5**	4 **4**	6× **1**
9+ **5**	**4**	**1**	**3**	**2**
1 **1**	20× **5**	1− **3**	2÷ **2**	**4**
4	**1**	**2**	2− **5**	**3**

Puzzle 67

+ − × ÷

1− **2**	9+ **5**	12× **4**	**3**	**1**
3	**4**	10× **1**	**2**	5 **5**
5+ **4**	18× **3**	**5**	2÷ **1**	**2**
1	**2**	**3**	9+ **5**	1− **4**
5 **5**	3+ **1**	**2**	**4**	**3**

Puzzle 68

+ − × ÷

5× **1**	**5**	7+ **2**	**3**	9+ **4**
1− **4**	**1**	3 **3**	**2**	**5**
3	3− **4**	**1**	4− **5**	6+ **2**
30× **5**	2÷ **2**	**4**	**1**	**3**
2	**3**	9+ **5**	**4**	**1**

Puzzle 69

+ − × ÷

9+ 5	2− 3	2÷ 1	2÷ 4	2
4	1	2	2− 5	3
2÷ 1	2	60× 4	3	4− 5
12× 3	4	5	2 2	1
3− 2	5	3 3	3− 1	4

Puzzle 70

+ − × ÷

1− 3	2÷ 2	9+ 5	4	4− 1
4	1	18× 2	3	5
1− 2	3	1	4− 5	4 4
9+ 5	4	3	1	1− 2
4− 1	5	2÷ 4	2	3

Puzzle 71

+ − × ÷

6× 2	3	4− 5	1	1− 4
1	6× 2	3	9+ 4	5
12× 4	2÷ 1	2	5	3 3
3	9+ 5	4	12× 2	1
1− 5	4	1 1	3	2

Puzzle 72

+ − × ÷

12× 4	3	4− 5	2÷ 2	1
3 3	11+ 5	1	2÷ 4	2
4− 1	4	2	2− 3	5
5	1− 2	3	4− 1	7+ 4
2÷ 2	1	4 4	5	3

Puzzle 73

+ − × ÷

3−	2−	3−	3+	4
5	**3**	**1**	**2**	**4**
2	**5**	**4**	**1**	15× **3**
2− **1**	4 **4**	5+ **2**	**3**	**5**
3	4− **1**	**5**	2÷ **4**	**2**
9+ **4**	**2**	**3**	4− **5**	**1**

Puzzle 74

+ − × ÷

3−	2÷		1	180×
5	**4**	**2**	**1**	**3**
2	**1**	4− **4**	**3**	**5**
1− **3**	**5**	7+ **1**	**2**	**4**
4	90× **2**	**3**	**5**	1− **1**
1 **1**	**3**	**5**	**4**	2÷ **2**

Puzzle 75

+ − × ÷

12×		9+	2÷	
4	**3**	**5**	**2**	**1**
1	10× **2**	**4**	4− **5**	7+ **3**
2− **3**	**5**	3+ **2**	**1**	**4**
5	8× **4**	**1**	72× **3**	**2**
2	**1**	**3**	**4**	5 **5**

Puzzle 76

+ − × ÷

3−	12×			4−
2	**1**	**3**	**4**	**5**
5	7+ **3**	**4**	6× **2**	**1**
15× **3**	**5**	7+ **2**	**1**	4 **4**
3− **1**	2÷ **4**	**5**	**3**	1− **2**
4	**2**	4− **1**	**5**	**3**

Puzzle 77

+ − × ÷

2− **1**	60× **5**	**4**	**3**	2 **2**
3	12× **4**	3+ **1**	2 **2**	15× **5**
2÷ **4**	**3**	**2**	20× **5**	**1**
2	2÷ **1**	2− **5**	**4**	**3**
5 **5**	**2**	**3**	5+ **1**	**4**

Puzzle 78

+ − × ÷

1− **5**	2÷ **2**	1 **1**	12× **4**	**3**
4	**1**	**2**	1− **3**	4− **5**
7+ **3**	9+ **4**	**5**	2 **2**	**1**
1	**3**	7+ **4**	4− **5**	2÷ **2**
7+ **2**	**5**	**3**	**1**	**4**

Puzzle 79

+ − × ÷

2÷ **2**	4− **5**	**1**	12× **3**	**4**
1	**2**	1− **3**	3 **4**	9+ **5**
1− **4**	**1**	3− **5**	**2**	3 **3**
3	7+ **4**	2− **2**	6+ **5**	2÷ **1**
5 **5**	**3**	**4**	**1**	**2**

Puzzle 80

+ − × ÷

80× **4**	**5**	3 **3**	1− **2**	3+ **1**
1− **1**	**4**	9+ **5**	**3**	**2**
2	2÷ **1**	**4**	8+ **5**	**3**
2− **3**	**2**	3− **1**	**4**	1− **5**
5	6× **3**	**2**	1 **1**	**4**

Puzzle 81

+ − × ÷

1−		12×		9+
3	**2**	**1**	**4**	**5**
7+			2÷	
2	**5**	**3**	**1**	**4**
5+		11+		18×
1	**4**	**5**	**2**	**3**
20×				
5	**1**	**4**	**3**	**2**
	3		4−	
4	**3**	**2**	**5**	**1**

Puzzle 82

+ − × ÷

3	3+		20×	
3	**1**	**2**	**4**	**5**
2÷	180×			
2	**3**	**4**	**5**	**1**
	5	10×		1−
4	**5**	**1**	**3**	**2**
4−	2÷			
1	**4**	**5**	**2**	**3**
		12×		
5	**2**	**3**	**1**	**4**

Puzzle 83

+ − × ÷

1−	2÷		20×	
3	**1**	**2**	**5**	**4**
	2−		12+	4−
2	**3**	**5**	**4**	**1**
2÷		4		
1	**2**	**4**	**3**	**5**
13+		4+		
5	**4**	**1**	**2**	**3**
	5		2÷	
4	**5**	**3**	**1**	**2**

Puzzle 84

+ − × ÷

4−		3	120×	
1	**5**	**3**	**4**	**2**
9+	2÷			
4	**1**	**2**	**3**	**5**
	12×	4−	6×	
5	**4**	**1**	**2**	**3**
6×				10+
2	**3**	**5**	**1**	**4**
	2÷			
3	**2**	**4**	**5**	**1**

Puzzle 85

+ − × ÷

24X 3	4	2	15X 5	1
2÷ 4	4− 5	1	3+ 2	3
2	2− 3	12X 4	1	3− 5
50X 5	1	3	11+ 4	2
1	2	5	3	4

Puzzle 86

+ − × ÷

4− 1	5	2÷ 2	4	8+ 3
3− 2	2÷ 4	45X 3	5	1
5	2	1	4− 3	4
11+ 4	3	5	20X 1	2
3	1	4 4	2	5

Puzzle 87

+ − × ÷

2÷ 1	2	4− 5	13+ 3	4 4
2÷ 4	12X 3	1	2	4− 5
2	4	3	5	1
4− 5	1	96X 2	4	3
2− 3	5	4	1− 1	2

Puzzle 88

+ − × ÷

18X 2	1− 4	3	4− 1	5
1	3	3− 5	2÷ 4	2
3	1 1	2	2− 5	3− 4
1− 5	2÷ 2	4	3	1
4	5	4− 1	5+ 2	3

Puzzle 89

+ − × ÷

3− 5	3+ 2	1	36× 3	60× 4
2	11+ 5	3	4	1
1 1	4	2	5	3
60× 4	3	5	2÷ 1	2
2− 3	1	2÷ 4	2	5 5

Puzzle 90

+ − × ÷

4 4	3+ 1	2	75× 5	3
3+ 2	5+ 3	4− 1	48× 4	5
1	2	5	3	4
15× 3	13+ 5	4	1 1	2÷ 2
5	4	5+ 3	2	1

Puzzle 91

+ − × ÷

24× 3	4	2	4− 1	5
1 1	2− 3	5	2÷ 4	2
2÷ 2	1	9+ 4	5	12× 3
3− 5	2	9× 1	3	4
20× 4	5	3	2÷ 2	1

Puzzle 92

+ − × ÷

1− 4	5	6× 1	1− 3	2
4− 1	9+ 4	3	2	20× 5
5	3	2	4− 1	4
3 3	2÷ 2	4	5	4+ 1
2÷ 2	1	9+ 5	4	3

Puzzle 93

+ − × ÷

2− 3	1	2− 5	2÷ 4	3− 2
4− 1	12+ 4	3	2	5
5	3	2÷ 2	3− 1	4
16× 2	5	4	2− 3	1
4	2	1 1	8+ 5	3

Puzzle 94

+ − × ÷

2÷ 2	1	20× 4	5	5+ 3
12+ 3	4− 5	1	5+ 4	2
5	1− 3	3− 2	1	3− 4
4	2	5	10+ 3	1
5+ 1	4	3 3	2	5

Puzzle 95

+ − × ÷

2− 1	3	6× 2	15+ 4	5
2 2	1	3	15× 5	4
20× 4	5	1	3	2
60× 3	4	3− 5	2	3× 1
5	2÷ 2	4	1	3

Puzzle 96

+ − × ÷

2÷ 2	1	9+ 4	5	30× 3
4− 1	2÷ 4	2	1− 3	5
5	1− 3	4− 1	4	2
3 3	2	5	2÷ 1	3− 4
12+ 4	5	3	2	1

Puzzle 97

+ − × ÷

4 4	**1** 4−	**5**	**2** 6×	**3**
1 8+	**4**	**3**	**5** 4−	**2** 2÷
5 8+	**3** 1−	**2**	**1**	**4**
3	**2** 7+	**1**	**4** 1−	**5** 4−
2 7+	**5**	**4**	**3**	**1**

Puzzle 98

+ − × ÷

2 1−	**4** 12×	**1**	**3**	**5** 4−
3	**5** 12+	**2** 2÷	**4**	**1**
5	**2**	**4** 12+	**1** 4−	**3** 3
4 5+	**1** 2−	**3**	**5**	**2** 16×
1	**3**	**5**	**2**	**4**

Puzzle 99

+ − × ÷

2 2÷	**1**	**5** 75×	**3**	**4** 2−
3 8+	**4** 5+	**1**	**5**	**2**
5	**2** 2÷	**4**	**1** 4+	**3**
4 12+	**5**	**3**	**2** 10×	**1**
1 2−	**3**	**2** 2−	**4**	**5**

Puzzle 100

+ − × ÷

1 4−	**4** 1−	**3**	**2** 2÷	**5** 5
5	**3** 6×	**2**	**4**	**1** 5+
2 2÷	**1** 6+	**5**	**3** 15×	**4**
4	**2** 2	**1** 3−	**5**	**3** 1−
3 2−	**5**	**4**	**1**	**2**

Puzzle 101

+ − × ÷

60×		6+		1
3	**5**	**2**	**4**	**1**
4	**1**	**5**	**2**	**3**
2÷			12×	
2	**4**	**1**	**3**	**5**
4−	6×			
5	**3**	**4**	**1**	**2**
		3	9+	
1	**2**	**3**	**5**	**4**

Puzzle 102

+ − × ÷

12×			3−	
4	**3**	**1**	**5**	**2**
2÷		6×	6+	
2	**4**	**3**	**1**	**5**
2−			2÷	4+
5	**1**	**2**	**4**	**3**
	20×			
3	**5**	**4**	**2**	**1**
3+		12+		
1	**2**	**5**	**3**	**4**

Puzzle 103

+ − × ÷

4−		20×	2÷	1−
1	**5**	**4**	**2**	**3**
2÷	5+			
2	**3**	**5**	**1**	**4**
			7+	7+
4	**2**	**1**	**3**	**5**
60×	1	1−		
5	**1**	**3**	**4**	**2**
			4−	
3	**4**	**2**	**5**	**1**

Puzzle 104

+ − × ÷

2−		12×	3−	3−
3	**5**	**4**	**2**	**1**
2	2÷			
2	**1**	**3**	**5**	**4**
3−		6+		2−
4	**2**	**5**	**1**	**3**
	3	2÷		
1	**3**	**2**	**4**	**5**
20×			1−	
5	**4**	**1**	**3**	**2**

Puzzle 105

+ − × ÷

8× **2**	12+ **5**	**3**	**4**	1 **1**
4	2 **2**	4− **5**	**1**	2− **3**
1	5+ **4**	1− **2**	**3**	**5**
3 **3**	**1**	5+ **4**	3− **5**	2÷ **2**
2− **5**	**3**	**1**	**2**	**4**

Puzzle 106

+ − × ÷

3+ **2**	4− **5**	**1**	12× **3**	1− **4**
1	**2**	1− **3**	**4**	**5**
20× **5**	**4**	2÷ **2**	**1**	6+ **3**
1− **3**	**1**	20× **4**	**5**	**2**
4	3 **3**	3− **5**	**2**	**1**

Puzzle 107

+ − × ÷

6+ **1**	**2**	120× **3**	**4**	**5**
3	4− **1**	**5**	**2**	40× **4**
60× **4**	**3**	2÷ **1**	**5**	**2**
5	20× **4**	**2**	7+ **3**	**1**
2 **2**	**5**	3− **4**	**1**	**3**

Puzzle 108

+ − × ÷

2÷ **2**	**4**	25× **5**	7+ **3**	1− **1**
3 **3**	**5**	**1**	**4**	**2**
1− **4**	4+ **3**	1− **2**	**1**	5 **5**
5	**1**	**3**	1− **2**	2÷ **4**
2÷ **1**	**2**	**4**	2− **5**	**3**

Puzzle 109

+ − × ÷

9+ 4	6× 3	2÷ 1	2	6+ 5
5	2	11+ 3	4	1
3− 2	5	4	9+ 1	3
2− 3	5+ 1	3− 2	5	24× 4
1	4	5	3	2

Puzzle 110

+ − × ÷

12+ 4	5	3	2÷ 2	1
2÷ 2	4	6× 1	4− 5	1− 3
9+ 5	3	2	1	4
3	4− 1	5	2÷ 4	2
1	2− 2	4	8+ 3	5

Puzzle 111

+ − × ÷

2− 1	2− 3	2÷ 4	2	10× 5
3	5	1 1	20× 4	2
9+ 4	1− 1	1− 2	5	1− 3
5	2	3	3× 1	4
11+ 2	4	5	3	1

Puzzle 112

+ − × ÷

6+ 2	4− 5	12× 3	1	4
3	1	1− 5	4	30× 2
1	2÷ 2	4	5	3
1− 5	8+ 4	2 2	4+ 3	1
4	3	1	7+ 2	5

Puzzle 113

+ − × ÷

4−	3	3+		24×
5	**3**	**2**	**1**	**4**
	1−			
1	**4**	**5**	**2**	**3**
2−		40×		
3	**1**	**4**	**5**	**2**
2÷	2−		1−	4−
2	**5**	**3**	**4**	**1**
	2÷			
4	**2**	**1**	**3**	**5**

Puzzle 114

+ − × ÷

4−	2	12×		
5	**2**	**4**	**1**	**3**
		2−	1−	5+
1	**3**	**5**	**2**	**4**
2÷	4−	1−		
4	**5**	**2**	**3**	**1**
			200×	
2	**1**	**3**	**4**	**5**
1−		1		
3	**4**	**1**	**5**	**2**

Puzzle 115

+ − × ÷

60×		6+		30×
3	**4**	**1**	**5**	**2**
2			12×	
2	**1**	**5**	**4**	**3**
4−	1−	2÷		
1	**2**	**4**	**3**	**5**
				5+
5	**3**	**2**	**1**	**4**
1−		5+		
4	**5**	**3**	**2**	**1**

Puzzle 116

+ − × ÷

2÷		15×		
4	**2**	**5**	**3**	**1**
8+			3−	1−
1	**3**	**4**	**2**	**5**
1−	2÷			
3	**1**	**2**	**5**	**4**
2	9+		3−	6×
2	**5**	**1**	**4**	**3**
20×				
5	**4**	**3**	**1**	**2**

Puzzle 117

				+−×÷
2− **3**	**1**	2÷ **4**	**2**	15+ **5**
8× **1**	1− **4**	**3**	**5**	**2**
2	3− **5**	3− **1**	**4**	**3**
4	**2**	3− **5**	4+ **3**	3− **1**
2− **5**	**3**	**2**	**1**	**4**

Puzzle 118

				+−×÷
9+ **2**	**5**	15× **1**	**3**	5+ **4**
3 **3**	**2**	10+ **4**	**5**	**1**
4− **5**	**4**	**2**	2− **1**	**3**
1	12× **3**	10+ **5**	2÷ **4**	**2**
4	**1**	**3**	**2**	5 **5**

Puzzle 119

				+−×÷
20× **1**	**4**	**5**	5+ **2**	**3**
1− **3**	**2**	20× **1**	**5**	**4**
40× **2**	3− **1**	**4**	2− **3**	**5**
5	15× **3**	2÷ **2**	**4**	2÷ **1**
4	**5**	2− **3**	**1**	**2**

Puzzle 120

				+−×÷
1− **3**	8× **2**	**4**	6+ **5**	**1**
2	5 **5**	**1**	2÷ **4**	7+ **3**
20× **1**	2− **3**	**5**	**2**	**4**
5	1− **4**	**3**	8+ **1**	**2**
4	6+ **1**	**2**	**3**	**5**

Puzzle 121

+ − × ÷

4− 5	1	1− 3	4	12× 2
2÷ 1	1− 4	9+ 5	2	3
2	5	1	3	10+ 4
7+ 3	11+ 2	4	5	1
4	6+ 3	2	1	5

Puzzle 122

+ − × ÷

1− 4	5	10× 2	2− 3	1
2− 3	1	5	9+ 2	4
2÷ 2	4	6+ 1	1− 5	3
15× 1	2	3	4	5 5
5	3	8× 4	1	2

Puzzle 123

+ − × ÷

3− 4	1− 2	2÷ 1	15× 3	5
1	3	2	1− 5	4
10+ 5	1− 4	3	2÷ 1	2
2	20× 1	40× 5	4	2− 3
3	5	4	2	1

Puzzle 124

+ − × ÷

48× 4	3	4− 1	3− 5	2
1	4	5	6+ 2	3
2 2	4− 5	1− 3	4	1
10+ 5	1	2÷ 2	12× 3	4
3	2	4	4− 1	5

Puzzle 125

				+ − × ÷	
10× 2	5	2− 6	4	3÷ 1	3
5− 6	12× 4	3	3+ 1	2	3− 5
1	2÷ 6	3− 4	10× 5	2− 3	2
12× 4	3	1	2	5	5− 6
3	8+ 2	5 5	36× 6	96× 4	1
5	1	2	3	6	4

Puzzle 126

				+ − × ÷	
3+ 2	1	40× 5	2÷ 3	24× 6	4
3÷ 1	2	4	6	15× 3	11+ 5
3	1− 4	5− 1	7+ 2	5	6
2− 4	3	6	5	5+ 1	6× 2
6	10+ 5	2	5+ 1	4	3
30× 5	6	3	4	2÷ 2	1

Puzzle 127

				+ − × ÷	
2÷ 2	2− 6	4	6+ 1	5	45× 3
4	3− 1	11+ 2	6	3	5
11+ 5	4	3	5+ 2	5− 6	1
6	1− 2	11+ 5	3	1	2÷ 4
2− 1	3	6	5 5	32× 4	2
3	4− 5	1	4	2	6 6

Puzzle 128

				+ − × ÷	
11+ 6	13+ 4	3+ 2	1	15× 3	5
5	3	6	2÷ 2	4	1
2÷ 2	5 5	18× 3	6	1	7+ 4
4	2÷ 2	4− 1	5	3÷ 6	3
2− 3	1	15+ 5	7+ 4	2	3÷ 6
1	6	4	3	5 5	2

Puzzle 129

+ − × ÷

11+ 6	5	2− 2	120× 4	5+ 3	1
30× 5	3	4	6	1	3÷ 2
2÷ 1	2	15× 3	5	19+ 4	6
2	3− 1	5	6× 3	6	4
3 3	4	5− 6	1	10+ 2	5
24× 4	6	1	2	5	3

Puzzle 130

+ − × ÷

5− 6	5	4	3÷ 3	1	10× 2
1	1− 2	6	9+ 4	3	5
3− 3	6	5 5	2	3− 4	1
40× 5	1− 3	2	1	5− 6	72× 4
4	1	3÷ 3	5	3− 2	6
2	4	1	11+ 6	5	3

Puzzle 131

+ − × ÷

60× 4	5	18× 1	3	60× 2	6
3+ 2	3	6	1 1	5	60× 4
1	48× 6	2	4	3	5
15× 5	24× 4	3	2	5− 6	1
3	1	100× 5	48× 6	4	2
3÷ 6	2	4	5	3÷ 1	3

Puzzle 132

+ − × ÷

6× 3	5− 1	24× 6	15× 5	2÷ 2	4
2	6	4	3	1	30× 5
1	2	1− 3	60× 4	5	6
11+ 6	3	10+ 5	1	4	6× 2
5	80× 4	2÷ 1	3÷ 2	10+ 6	3
4	5	2	6	3	1

Puzzle 133

$+ - \times \div$

4 <small>12×</small>	**6** <small>2÷</small>	**3**	**5** <small>7+</small>	**2**	**1** <small>5−</small>
3	**1** <small>1</small>	**2** <small>2÷</small>	**4** <small>15+</small>	**5**	**6**
2 <small>6×</small>	**3**	**4**	**6**	**1** <small>4−</small>	**5**
5 <small>3−</small>	**2**	**6** <small>5−</small>	**1**	**4** <small>1−</small>	**3**
6 <small>5−</small>	**5** <small>1−</small>	**1** <small>2÷</small>	**2**	**3** <small>2÷</small>	**4** <small>2÷</small>
1	**4**	**5** <small>15×</small>	**3**	**6**	**2**

Puzzle 134

$+ - \times \div$

5 <small>20×</small>	**6** <small>3÷</small>	**2** <small>5+</small>	**1** <small>5−</small>	**3** <small>2−</small>	**4** <small>4</small>
4	**2**	**3**	**6**	**5**	**1** <small>3÷</small>
1	**5** <small>1−</small>	**4**	**2** <small>4−</small>	**6**	**3**
3 <small>12×</small>	**4**	**1** <small>5−</small>	**5** <small>8+</small>	**2** <small>240×</small>	**6**
2 <small>2</small>	**1**	**6**	**3**	**4**	**5**
6 <small>14+</small>	**3**	**5** <small>7+</small>	**4**	**1**	**2**

Puzzle 135

$+ - \times \div$

1 <small>10×</small>	**5**	**2**	**3** <small>3÷</small>	**4** <small>1−</small>	**6** <small>3÷</small>
5 <small>8+</small>	**4** <small>2÷</small>	**6** <small>10+</small>	**1**	**3**	**2**
3	**2**	**4**	**6** <small>5−</small>	**1**	**5** <small>60×</small>
4 <small>2÷</small>	**6** <small>5−</small>	**3** <small>2−</small>	**5** <small>3−</small>	**2**	**1**
2	**1**	**5**	**4** <small>2÷</small>	**6** <small>30×</small>	**3**
6 <small>18×</small>	**3**	**1**	**2**	**5**	**4**

Puzzle 136

$+ - \times \div$

6 <small>2−</small>	**4**	**5** <small>3−</small>	**2**	**1** <small>3×</small>	**3**
2 <small>3+</small>	**6** <small>24×</small>	**4**	**3** <small>15×</small>	**5**	**1**
1	**5** <small>3−</small>	**3** <small>3÷</small>	**4** <small>2÷</small>	**2**	**6** <small>2−</small>
5 <small>8+</small>	**2**	**1** <small>2÷</small>	**6**	**3**	**4**
3	**1** <small>5−</small>	**6**	**5** <small>20×</small>	**4**	**2** <small>13+</small>
4 <small>1−</small>	**3**	**2** <small>2÷</small>	**1**	**6**	**5**

Puzzle 137

+ − × ÷

2÷ 2	2− 3	1	8+ 5	24× 6	4
1	5− 6	2÷ 4	3	2	3− 5
1− 3	1	2	20× 4	5	3÷ 6
4	360× 5	3	5− 6	1	2
30× 5	4	6	20× 2	3÷ 3	1
6	2	5	1	12× 4	3

Puzzle 138

+ − × ÷

5− 6	12× 2	12× 3	4	10+ 5	1
1	3	2	3− 5	4	1− 6
72× 3	4	6	2	3÷ 1	5
200× 5	3− 1	4	6× 6	3	12× 2
4	11+ 6	5	1	2	3
2	5	3÷ 1	3	10+ 6	4

Puzzle 139

+ − × ÷

1− 3	2	2÷ 4	11+ 6	6+ 1	5
12× 4	3	2	5	5− 6	1
11+ 6	5	3− 1	4	7+ 2	3
5 5	120× 4	5− 6	1	10+ 3	2
2÷ 2	1	5	3	4	24× 6
1	6	5+ 3	2	5 5	4

Puzzle 140

+ − × ÷

3− 5	2	4	72× 6	3	5− 1
3÷ 1	3 3	20× 5	40× 2	4	6
3	4	1	5	11+ 6	1− 2
3÷ 2	5− 1	6	4 4	5	3
6	2− 5	3	3+ 1	2	1− 4
2− 4	6	6× 2	3	1	5

Puzzle 141

+ − × ÷

3÷ 1	3	11+ 5	6	2÷ 2	4
8× 2	1	2÷ 3	9+ 4	5	6 6
4	2÷ 2	6	2− 3	1	2− 5
11+ 5	4	2− 2	5− 1	6	3
6	5 5	4	1− 2	3	2÷ 1
2÷ 3	6	6+ 1	5	4 4	2

Puzzle 142

+ − × ÷

75× 5	9+ 2	6	1	3 3	5+ 4
3	5	3+ 2	2− 4	6	1
1− 2	3	1	1− 5	4	3÷ 6
5− 1	6	4	8+ 3	5	2
96× 6	4	3	3+ 2	1	15× 5
4	1 1	60× 5	6	2	3

Puzzle 143

+ − × ÷

2− 3	5	5− 1	6	2÷ 4	2
16× 2	9+ 4	5	5− 1	6	9× 3
4	2	3÷ 6	2− 5	3	1
1− 5	6	2	3	3− 1	4
5− 6	3÷ 1	3	2− 4	2	30× 5
1	1− 3	4	7+ 2	5	6

Puzzle 144

+ − × ÷

4− 5	5− 6	1	2÷ 2	4	1− 3
1	5	1− 4	6	2÷ 3	2
3+ 2	1	3	1− 4	120× 6	5
3 3	3÷ 2	6	5× 1	5	4
2− 4	7+ 3	10× 2	2− 5	1	5− 6
6	4	5	3	2 2	1

Puzzle 145

$+ - \times \div$

2− 5	3	1− 2	5− 6	5+ 1	4
5− 6	3÷ 2	3	1	1− 4	10× 5
1	6	9+ 4	7+ 5	3	2
9+ 4	3− 1	5	2	11+ 6	18× 3
2	4	3÷ 1	3	5	6
3	11+ 5	6	2÷ 4	2	1

Puzzle 146

$+ - \times \div$

3− 1	1− 2	3	6	1− 5	12× 4
4	5	7+ 2	1	5− 6	3
7+ 3	4	7+ 5	2	5− 1	6
3÷ 2	5− 6	1	12× 4	3	10× 5
6	3	2− 4	20× 5	2− 2	1
5 5	1	2÷ 6	3	4	2

Puzzle 147

$+ - \times \div$

4− 5	1	1− 6	3 3	2− 4	2
3÷ 1	3÷ 2	5	8× 4	1− 3	11+ 6
3	6	7+ 4	1	2	5
1− 4	5	3	2	5− 6	1
3÷ 2	3− 4	1	11+ 6	5	7+ 3
6	5+ 3	2	6+ 5	1	4

Puzzle 148

$+ - \times \div$

20× 5	4	1	15+ 3	2	5− 6
13+ 2	5	3	6	4	1
3	48× 6	2	4	3÷ 1	20× 5
2− 6	2 2	4− 5	1	3	4
4	5− 1	6	10× 2	5	5+ 3
8+ 1	3	4	11+ 5	6	2

Puzzle 149

+ − × ÷

¹⁰ˣ 1	**5**	**²÷ 4**	**2**	**²÷ 3**	**6**
2	**⁵⁻ 1**	**6**	**²⁻ 4**	**⁹⁺ 5**	**³÷ 3**
¹²⁰ˣ 5	**¹⁻ 3**	**2**	**6**	**4**	**1**
6	**³⁻ 2**	**5**	**³÷ 3**	**³⁺ 1**	**¹⁻ 4**
4	**²¹⁶ˣ 6**	**3**	**1**	**2**	**5**
3	**4**	**⁴⁻ 1**	**5**	**³÷ 6**	**2**

Puzzle 150

+ − × ÷

⁶⁰ˣ 5	**4**	**1**	**³ 3**	**³÷ 2**	**6**
⁸ˣ 2	**³÷ 1**	**3**	**²¹⁺ 4**	**6**	**⁵ 5**
4	**3**	**¹⁴⁺ 2**	**6**	**5**	**³ˣ 1**
⁵⁻ 6	**⁵ 5**	**4**	**¹²⁰ˣ 2**	**1**	**3**
1	**2**	**6**	**5**	**3**	**4**
³ 3	**¹¹⁺ 6**	**5**	**⁸ˣ 1**	**4**	**2**

Puzzle 151

+ − × ÷

¹¹⁺ 5	**6**	**² 2**	**⁶ˣ 1**	**3**	**¹²ˣ 4**
³⁻ 4	**1**	**¹¹⁺ 5**	**6**	**2**	**3**
²÷ 1	**4**	**⁵⁴ˣ 6**	**3**	**¹⁰ˣ 5**	**2**
2	**5**	**3**	**⁸⁰ˣ 4**	**⁵⁻ 1**	**6**
⁵⁺ 3	**2**	**4**	**5**	**¹⁰⁺ 6**	**⁶⁺ 1**
³⁻ 6	**3**	**³⁺ 1**	**2**	**4**	**5**

Puzzle 152

+ − × ÷

³÷ 1	**3**	**⁶ˣ 2**	**6**	**⁵⁻ 5**	**¹⁻ 4**
¹³⁺ 5	**4**	**3**	**1**	**³÷ 2**	**6**
4	**²⁴ˣ 6**	**1**	**5**	**²⁻ 3**	**² 2**
³⁺ 2	**1**	**4**	**⁹⁰ˣ 3**	**6**	**5**
²÷ 3	**³⁻ 5**	**¹⁵⁺ 6**	**² 2**	**³⁻ 4**	**³÷ 1**
6	**2**	**5**	**4**	**1**	**3**

Puzzle 153

+ − × ÷

1− 2	60× 5	3	5+ 4	1	3÷ 6
3	15+ 6	4	1	5 5	2
6	3	3− 2	5	3− 4	1
8× 1	4	2÷ 6	3	3− 2	5
20× 5	2	5− 1	6	10+ 3	4
4	4− 1	5	3÷ 2	6	3

Puzzle 154

+ − × ÷

1 1	120× 4	5	2÷ 2	36× 6	3
8+ 5	3	6	1	2	3− 4
12+ 4	6	2	15× 5	3	1
6+ 2	1	3	2− 6	4	1− 5
6× 3	2	3− 1	1− 4	10× 5	6
11+ 6	5	4	3	1	2

Puzzle 155

+ − × ÷

6+ 1	5	24× 3	10+ 4	3÷ 2	6
2− 6	4	2	5	3÷ 3	1
10× 5	2÷ 3	4	1	5− 6	2÷ 2
2	6	11+ 5	1− 3	1	4
3÷ 3	1	6	2	9+ 4	5
2÷ 4	2	5− 1	6	2− 5	3

Puzzle 156

+ − × ÷

3− 2	3 3	24× 4	6	12× 1	15× 5
5	6× 6	1	6+ 2	4	3
5− 6	1− 4	5	1	3	2− 2
1	5	3− 2	3	13+ 6	4
8+ 3	3÷ 2	6	4 4	5	5− 1
4	1	3	2− 5	2	6

Puzzle 157

+ − × ÷

2− 5	3	40× 2	1	10+ 4	6
3÷ 2	6	4	5	2− 3	1
5− 6	9+ 4	3	2	6+ 1	5 5
1	15+ 5	6	4	2	3
5+ 4	1	14+ 5	3	4− 6	2
6+ 3	2	1	6	9+ 5	4

Puzzle 158

+ − × ÷

144× 6	4	1− 1	5	2− 2	1− 3
12+ 4	6	2	3	5 5	8× 1
5	3	5− 6	1	4	2
2÷ 1	20× 5	4	5+ 2	3	1− 6
2	1	3÷ 3	4	24× 6	5
1− 3	2	30× 5	6	3− 1	4

Puzzle 159

+ − × ÷

3− 1	4	6× 3	2	1− 6	5
8+ 3	5	5− 6	3− 1	2÷ 2	4
1− 5	3÷ 6	1	4	8+ 3	2÷ 2
6	2	1− 4	3	5	1
7+ 4	3	3− 2	30× 5	5− 1	6
2÷ 2	1	5	6	1− 4	3

Puzzle 160

+ − × ÷

1− 4	20× 5	2÷ 1	3− 3	4− 6	2
3	4	2	6	11+ 1	1− 5
90× 5	6	3	5+ 1	2	4
8+ 2	1	5	4	3	5− 6
5− 6	5+ 3	2− 4	7+ 2	5	1
1	2	6	5	7+ 4	3

Puzzle 161

+ − × ÷

2÷		1−		1−		30×			
1	**2**	**3**	**4**	**6**	**5**
14+					5	6+	
6	**4**	**2**	**3**	**5**	**1**
	5−		5+		3−		
4	**6**	**1**	**5**	**2**	**3**
75×			3−				
5	**1**	**4**	**6**	**3**	**2**
		1−	2÷		3−		
3	**5**	**6**	**2**	**1**	**4**
1−				2−			
2	**3**	**5**	**1**	**4**	**6**

Puzzle 162

+ − × ÷

11+		6×	3÷		2−		
6	**5**	**3**	**1**	**2**	**4**
30×					11+		
1	**6**	**2**	**3**	**4**	**5**
	12×	2−		50×			
5	**3**	**6**	**4**	**1**	**2**
1−					2÷		
3	**1**	**4**	**2**	**5**	**6**
	32×			18×			
2	**4**	**1**	**5**	**6**	**3**
		11+					
4	**2**	**5**	**6**	**3**	**1**

Puzzle 163

+ − × ÷

1−	2−		3+		5−		
4	**5**	**3**	**2**	**1**	**6**
	24×		3÷	4−			
5	**6**	**4**	**3**	**2**	**1**
2÷		4−			15×		
2	**4**	**5**	**1**	**6**	**3**
1−			30×	1−			
3	**2**	**1**	**6**	**4**	**5**
5−	1−				2÷		
6	**1**	**2**	**5**	**3**	**4**
	2÷		1−				
1	**3**	**6**	**4**	**5**	**2**

Puzzle 164

+ − × ÷

6×	15+		3+		4−		
3	**6**	**4**	**2**	**1**	**5**
		3−		4			
2	**5**	**6**	**3**	**4**	**1**
9+		2÷	11+	11+			
4	**1**	**2**	**6**	**5**	**3**
5−					3÷		
6	**4**	**1**	**5**	**3**	**2**
	11+		7+				
1	**3**	**5**	**4**	**2**	**6**
3−				2−			
5	**2**	**3**	**1**	**6**	**4**

Puzzle 165

+ − × ÷

2−		6×		4−	
4	**6**	**2**	**3**	**5**	**1**
2÷		5−		2−	
2	**4**	**6**	**1**	**3**	**5**
5+	1−		4−		2÷
1	**5**	**4**	**2**	**6**	**3**
		8+	2−	2÷	
3	**1**	**5**	**4**	**2**	**6**
30×	2				2÷
5	**2**	**3**	**6**	**1**	**4**
	2−		1−		
6	**3**	**1**	**5**	**4**	**2**

Puzzle 166

+ − × ÷

40×		5−		24×	
2	**5**	**6**	**1**	**3**	**4**
15+		2−			6×
6	**4**	**3**	**5**	**2**	**1**
	2÷	3−		5−	
5	**3**	**1**	**4**	**6**	**2**
		7+			
4	**6**	**5**	**2**	**1**	**3**
4+		2−	3−	600×	
1	**2**	**4**	**3**	**5**	**6**
3					
3	**1**	**2**	**6**	**4**	**5**

Puzzle 167

+ − × ÷

2−	3−		11+	2÷	3÷
4	**5**	**2**	**6**	**1**	**3**
	1−				
6	**4**	**3**	**5**	**2**	**1**
2÷		12×		1−	
2	**1**	**4**	**3**	**6**	**5**
2÷		4−		2÷	
3	**6**	**5**	**1**	**4**	**2**
4−	3+		2÷	2−	2−
5	**2**	**1**	**4**	**3**	**6**
	3−				
1	**3**	**6**	**2**	**5**	**4**

Puzzle 168

+ − × ÷

72×	2÷		14+		
4	**6**	**3**	**2**	**5**	**1**
		1−	5−		
6	**3**	**5**	**1**	**2**	**4**
15×				2÷	
3	**5**	**4**	**6**	**1**	**2**
3+		3÷	2−	13+	
2	**1**	**6**	**5**	**4**	**3**
10×	4				14+
1	**4**	**2**	**3**	**6**	**5**
		5+			
5	**2**	**1**	**4**	**3**	**6**

Puzzle 169

				+ − × ÷	
2÷ 6	6+ 2	1	3	40× 5	4
3	5 5	14+ 4	5− 1	2	3÷ 6
4	1	5	6	3 3	2
15+ 1	3	2	12+ 4	6	6+ 5
3− 5	6	3	2	8+ 4	1
2	120× 4	6	5	1	3

Puzzle 170

				+ − × ÷	
3÷ 2	6	24× 4	1	2− 5	3
2− 5	3	1	6	2÷ 2	4
2÷ 4	2	1− 3	60× 5	5− 6	1
5− 6	15+ 4	2	3	3÷ 1	13+ 5
1	5	6	4	3	2
3 3	4− 1	5	2÷ 2	4	6

Puzzle 171

				+ − × ÷	
15× 5	1	2− 4	6	24× 2	3
3	5− 6	1	13+ 2	5	4
5− 6	1− 4	3	5	1	3− 2
1	1− 3	2	10+ 4	6	5
2÷ 2	11+ 5	6	36× 3	4	5− 1
4	8+ 2	5	1	3	6

Puzzle 172

				+ − × ÷	
30× 3	2	5	1− 1	13+ 6	4
4− 1	20+ 5	6	2	2÷ 4	3
5	6	3	48× 4	2	5− 1
2÷ 2	3÷ 1	4	3	4− 5	6
4	3	4− 2	6	1	30× 5
16+ 6	4	1	5	3	2

Puzzle 173

					+ − × ÷
30X 2	**5−** 1	6	**1−** 4	5	**2÷** 3
3	5	**2−** 4	**6+** 1	2	6
6+ 5	**3÷** 6	2	3	**10+** 4	**5+** 1
1	2	**2−** 3	**10X** 5	6	4
14+ 6	4	1	2	**18X** 3	**3−** 5
4	**2−** 3	5	6	1	2

Puzzle 174

					+ − × ÷
6X 3	2	**6+** 1	5	**6X** 6	**7+** 4
1− 4	**1−** 5	**3÷** 6	**1−** 3	1	2
5	6	2	4	**1−** 3	1
4− 6	**2−** 3	**1−** 4	**5−** 1	2	**14+** 5
2	1	5	6	**9+** 4	3
5+ 1	4	3	2	5	6

Puzzle 175

					+ − × ÷
6X 3	**4−** 5	1	**2÷** 2	4	**10+** 6
2	**2−** 6	4	**13+** 5	3	1
2÷ 6	3	5	1	2	**12X** 4
20X 5	4	**48X** 2	6	1	3
5+ 1	**5+** 2	3	4	**21+** 6	5
4	**5−** 1	6	3	5	2

Puzzle 176

					+ − × ÷
5− 6	**20X** 5	1	4	**3** 3	**1−** 2
1	4	**13+** 6	2	**12+** 5	3
6X 2	**2÷** 1	3	5	**5−** 6	**1−** 4
3	2	**17+** 4	**72X** 6	1	5
5	6	2	3	4	1
12+ 4	3	5	**2÷** 1	2	**6** 6

Puzzle 177

+ − × ÷

1− 2	1	60× 5	80× 4	3− 3	6
3− 3	6	2	5	4	3+ 1
6	12+ 4	2÷ 3	1− 1	10+ 5	2
5	3	6	2	1	4
1 1	7+ 2	4	2÷ 3	1− 6	5
20× 4	5	1	6	2	3

Puzzle 178

+ − × ÷

48× 3	4	5	6	1− 1	8+ 2
4	2÷ 1	5− 6	1− 3	7+ 2	5
11+ 6	2	1	4	5	2− 3
5	24× 6	4	6× 2	3	1
2÷ 1	1− 3	2	20× 5	4	2− 6
2	15+ 5	3	1	6	4

Puzzle 179

+ − × ÷

72× 4	2÷ 2	5− 6	1	2− 5	2− 3
6	4	8+ 5	48× 2	3	1
3	1	2	6	4	5 5
2÷ 1	3 3	1− 4	5	48× 2	6
2	16+ 5	2− 1	1− 3	9+ 6	4
5	6	3	4	1	2

Puzzle 180

+ − × ÷

2÷ 2	1− 6	5	3− 4	1	3− 3
1	5	1− 4	30× 2	3	6
2− 6	3 3	1− 2	6+ 1	5	3− 4
4	2− 2	3	5	4− 6	1
2− 3	4	5− 1	6	2	3− 5
5	1	5− 6	1− 3	4	2

Puzzle 181

					+ − × ÷
6 [1−]	4 [72X]	5 [5]	2 [2÷]	1 [2÷]	3 [2−]
5	6	3	4	2	1
2 [3+]	1	4 [13+]	3	5 [30X]	6
4 [1−]	5	1 [30X]	6	3 [1−]	2
3 [3÷]	2 [12X]	6	1	4 [24X]	5 [1−]
1	3	2	5	6	4

Puzzle 182

					+ − × ÷
4 [13+]	1 [3−]	2 [4−]	6	5 [2−]	3 [11+]
6	4	1 [1]	5 [40X]	3	2
3	5 [14+]	4	2	1	6
2 [1−]	3	5	4	6 [5−]	1
5 [1−]	6	3 [2÷]	1 [3÷]	2 [2−]	4
1 [3+]	2	6	3	4 [1−]	5

Puzzle 183

					+ − × ÷
5 [75X]	3	1 [2−]	6	4 [2−]	2 [9+]
2 [2÷]	5	3	1 [5−]	6	4
1	6 [3÷]	4 [2÷]	2	5 [2−]	3
6 [18+]	2	5 [1−]	4	3	1 [6+]
4	1	6 [3÷]	3 [1−]	2	5
3	4	2	5 [4−]	1	6 [6]

Puzzle 184

					+ − × ÷
6 [1−]	5	2 [3÷]	3 [1−]	4 [12X]	1
1 [5+]	4	6	2	3	5 [10+]
4 [2−]	6 [5−]	1 [13+]	5	2	3
2	1	3	4	5 [13+]	6
5 [2−]	3	4 [1−]	6 [5−]	1 [1]	2
3 [5+]	2	5	1	6 [2−]	4

Puzzle 185

+ − × ÷

2÷ 3	75× 5	3− 1	4	48× 6	2
6	3	5	3+ 1	2	4
18× 1	6	3	24× 2	4	6+ 5
48× 4	2	6	13+ 5	3	1
3− 2	9+ 1	4	3	5	10+ 6
5	4	3÷ 2	6	1	3

Puzzle 186

+ − × ÷

18× 1	6	2÷ 2	48× 4	2− 3	5
12+ 5	3	1	2	6	12× 4
2	5	15+ 4	6	1	3
48× 6	2	5	18+ 3	4 4	5− 1
4	12× 1	3	5	9+ 2	6
3	4	6	1	5	2

Puzzle 187

+ − × ÷

108× 3	2	6+ 5	1	48× 6	4
2÷ 1	3	6	1− 4	5	2
2	3÷ 1	3	6 6	1− 4	5
120× 4	4− 6	2	9+ 5	3	1
5	20× 4	1	6+ 3	2	2÷ 6
6	5	2÷ 4	2	1	3

Puzzle 188

+ − × ÷

15× 3	15+ 6	3− 4	1− 2	6+ 5	1
5	4	1	3	24× 6	2
1	5	1− 3	1− 6	2	4 4
12+ 4	6+ 1	2	5	360× 3	6
2	3	11+ 6	5+ 1	4	5
6	2	5	4	3÷ 1	3

Puzzle 189

+ − × ÷

2÷ 2	**5−** 6	1	**2−** 3	5	**12×** 4
1	**1−** 2	**20+** 5	6	**2÷** 4	3
1− 4	3	**3÷** 6	5	2	**12+** 1
3	**48×** 1	2	4	6	5
16+ 5	4	3	**2×** 2	1	**11+** 6
6	5	4	1	3	2

Puzzle 190

+ − × ÷

10× 5	2	**2−** 3	1	**2−** 4	6
9+ 1	3	5	**48×** 4	6	2
2÷ 3	**7+** 4	1	**13+** 6	2	**9+** 5
6	1	**5−** 2	5	**9+** 3	4
2 2	6	**144×** 4	3	5	1
20× 4	5	6	2	**3÷** 1	3

Puzzle 191

+ − × ÷

5− 1	6	**2÷** 2	5	**7+** 4	**1−** 3
54× 6	3	4	2	**12+** 1	5
3	**2÷** 2	1	**1−** 4	5	6
17+ 4	1	5	**108×** 3	6	2
2	**1−** 5	**2÷** 6	**5−** 1	3	**7+** 4
5	4	3	6	2	1

Puzzle 192

+ − × ÷

3− 2	5	**18×** 1	**7+** 4	**2÷** 3	6
2− 5	6	3	2	1	**2÷** 4
3	**5−** 1	6	**9+** 5	4	2
6 6	**10+** 4	2	**15+** 1	5	3
3÷ 1	3	4	6	**3−** 2	5
2÷ 4	2	**2−** 5	3	**5−** 6	1

Puzzle 193

+ − × ÷

90X 3	5	**5−** 6	1	**2÷** 2	4
6	**14+** 3	5	2	4	**5−** 1
1 1	**60X** 2	**180X** 3	4	**10X** 5	6
5	6	**3−** 4	3	1	2
2÷ 2	4	1	5	**3−** 6	3
3− 4	1	**3÷** 2	6	**2−** 3	5

Puzzle 194

+ − × ÷

3÷ 2	**1−** 3	4	**3÷** 1	**600X** 5	6
6	**2÷** 1	2	3	4	5
9+ 4	5	**3÷** 1	**3÷** 6	2	**1−** 3
30X 5	6	3	2	**1−** 1	4
3÷ 1	**2−** 4	6	5	**1−** 3	**11+** 2
3	**3−** 2	5	4	6	**1** 1

Puzzle 195

+ − × ÷

30X 2	5	**3** 3	**5−** 6	**10+** 4	1
15+ 6	3	**3÷** 2	1	5	**9+** 4
4	**6X** 1	6	**10X** 5	2	3
5	6	1	**1−** 4	3	2
2÷ 1	2	**9+** 4	**1−** 3	**1−** 6	5
1− 3	4	5	2	**5−** 1	6

Puzzle 196

+ − × ÷

5− 6	**2÷** 4	2	**2−** 3	1	**3−** 5
1	**12X** 3	4	**15+** 5	6	2
16+ 5	6	1	4	**8+** 2	3
12X 2	5	**6X** 6	1	3	**9+** 4
3	2	**2−** 5	**3÷** 6	4	1
5+ 4	1	3	2	**1−** 5	6

Puzzle 197

+ − × ÷

144X 6	4− 1	5	24X 4	2	3
2	3	10+ 1	5	4	11+ 6
4	2÷ 2	2÷ 6	5− 1	2− 3	5
24+ 1	4	3	6	5	2÷ 2
5	6	6+ 2	3	1	4
3	5	12X 4	2	6	1

Puzzle 198

+ − × ÷

2÷ 1	2	15+ 5	6	4	12X 3
360X 6	5	3	2÷ 2	1	4
4	3÷ 6	2	1	15X 3	5
10+ 2	2÷ 3	6	1− 4	6+ 5	1
3	4	1	5	24X 2	6
4− 5	1	13+ 4	3	6	2

Puzzle 199

+ − × ÷

36X 2	6	1− 4	2÷ 1	2− 5	3
8+ 1	3	5	2	2÷ 6	4 4
6	1	2÷ 2	4	3	3− 5
14+ 4	5	2÷ 3	6	24X 1	2
5	24X 2	6X 1	2− 3	4	6
3	4	6	5	2÷ 2	1

Puzzle 200

+ − × ÷

3÷ 2	6	15X 5	3	3− 1	4
12+ 3	2	4	1	120X 6	2− 5
15+ 6	1	2	5	4	3
4	90X 5	6	7+ 2	3	14+ 1
5	3	1 1	72X 4	2	6
3− 1	4	3	6	5	2

Puzzle 201

+ − × ÷

12×			16+		30×
4	3	1	5	6	2
3−		144×			
5	2	6	1	4	3
3÷			2÷	18+	
1	6	4	3	2	5
	11+				
3	1	2	6	5	4
2			2÷	2−	
2	5	3	4	1	6
15+					
6	4	5	2	3	1

Puzzle 202

+ − × ÷

2÷	5−		2÷	3−	4−
4	1	6	3	2	5
	24×				
2	4	3	6	5	1
4−		15+			7+
1	2	4	5	6	3
		3÷		3÷	
5	6	2	1	3	4
2÷	2−			3−	4−
6	3	5	4	1	2
		4−		2−	
3	5	1	2	4	6

Puzzle 203

+ − × ÷

6×		7+		7+	
1	6	4	3	2	5
2÷	3÷		1−		2−
6	3	1	4	5	2
		3−		5−	
3	5	2	1	6	4
2−		1−		3÷	
2	4	5	6	3	1
20×		3÷		72×	
5	1	6	2	4	3
	5+		6+		
4	2	3	5	1	6

Puzzle 204

+ − × ÷

24×			3	3−	
4	6	1	3	5	2
4−	2÷	2÷	2÷		2−
5	4	6	1	2	3
			2÷	5−	
1	2	3	4	6	5
2÷	4−	2−			2−
3	5	4	2	1	6
			90×		
6	1	2	5	3	4
10+				3−	
2	3	5	6	4	1

Puzzle 205

					+ − × ÷
90X 6	5	48X 3	12+ 4	2	1
3	2	4	2÷ 6	6X 1	5
3− 5	5− 1	2	3	6	12X 4
2	6	12+ 5	2÷ 1	1− 4	3
48X 4	3	1	2	5	180X 6
1	4	6	5	3	2

Puzzle 206

					+ − × ÷
20X 5	2	2÷ 6	3	24X 4	3÷ 1
2	15+ 5	4	6	1	3
2÷ 3	4− 1	5	2÷ 2	6	1− 4
6	3÷ 3	1	4	10+ 2	5
16X 4	10+ 6	3	1	5	3÷ 2
1	4	3− 2	5	3	6

Puzzle 207

+ − × ÷

20× 4	6− 7	10× 5	3÷ 2	13+ 6	8+ 1	3
5	1	2	6	7	5+ 3	4
3 3	24× 4	6− 7	1	9+ 5	2	13+ 6
3+ 2	3	4− 1	5	4	13+ 6	7
1	2	72× 6	4	3	7	25× 5
13+ 7	11+ 6	12× 4	21× 3	2÷ 2	5	1
6	5	3	7	1	2÷ 4	2

Puzzle 208

+ − × ÷

2 2	15+ 5	6× 3	1	1− 4	20+ 7	6
3	7	2	3− 4	5	6	1
168× 4	18+ 2	5	7	8+ 6	1	17+ 3
7	24× 4	6	5	1	2− 3	2
1	6	24× 4	2	3	5	7
6	6− 1	7	2÷ 3	2÷ 2	4	5
15× 5	3	1	6	7 7	2÷ 2	4

Puzzle 209

+ − × ÷

2−		10×			24+		
3	**1**	**2**	**5**	**6**	**4**	**7**
3÷ **6**	1− **4**	12+ **1**	**7**	21× **3**	**2**	**5**
2	**5**	**4**	**1**	**7**	2÷ **3**	**6**
6× **1**	**6**	5 **5**	2− **2**	**4**	10+ **7**	**3**
3− **4**	6× **3**	126× **7**	60× **6**	**2**	4− **5**	**1**
7	**2**	**6**	**3**	**5**	8× **1**	**4**
12+ **5**	**7**	1− **3**	**4**	5− **1**	**6**	**2**

Puzzle 210

+ − × ÷

112×		12+	18×		3−	
7	**4**	**3**	**6**	**1**	**5**	**2**
4	**7**	**2**	**3**	12+ **6**	**1**	**5**
10+ **2**	20× **1**	**4**	**5**	3 **3**	3528× **7**	**6**
3	18+ **6**	**5**	**7**	2÷ **2**	**4**	1 **1**
5	9+ **2**	**6**	**1**	**4**	**3**	**7**
18× **6**	35× **5**	**1**	11+ **4**	12+ **7**	**2**	**3**
1	**3**	**7**	**2**	**5**	2− **6**	**4**

Puzzle 211

+ − × ÷

210× 1	6	7	1− 2	12+ 5	3	4
20+ 4	1− 3	5	1	196× 7	3÷ 6	2
5	2	2÷ 3	6	1	4	7
6	24+ 7	12+ 4	5	3	6+ 2	1 1
2	5	13+ 6	7	24× 4	1	3
3	1	2÷ 2	1− 4	6	2− 7	5
7	4	1	3	13+ 2	5	6

Puzzle 212

+ − × ÷

288× 4	6	3	23+ 2	7	4− 1	5
12× 1	4	2	3 3	5	19+ 6	7
3	2	1	42× 7	4	5	6
10× 2	12+ 5	7	6	7+ 3	4	3− 1
5	8+ 7	1− 6	1	3÷ 2	1− 3	4
1− 7	1	5	1− 4	6	2	1− 3
6	1− 3	4	5	6− 1	7	2

Puzzle 213

+ − × ÷

1− **4**	28× **7**	**2**	14+ **5**	**3**	**1**	5− **6**
3	**2**	2÷ **6**	5+ **4**	1− **7**	**5**	**1**
2÷ **2**	15× **5**	**3**	**1**	**6**	3− **4**	5− **7**
1	**3**	480× **4**	**6**	**5**	**7**	**2**
11+ **5**	**6**	6− **1**	**7**	**4**	1− **2**	**3**
1− **7**	12+ **1**	30× **5**	**3**	**2**	2÷ **6**	1− **4**
6	**4**	**7**	2÷ **2**	**1**	**3**	**5**

Puzzle 214

+ − × ÷

1− **5**	2÷ **4**	**2**	42× **6**	**1**	**7**	8+ **3**
4	6− **1**	**7**	1− **3**	3÷ **6**	**2**	**5**
2÷ **1**	**2**	13+ **3**	**4**	15+ **7**	1− **5**	**6**
5− **7**	**6**	**4**	1 **1**	**5**	**3**	2÷ **2**
2	8+ **3**	**5**	9+ **7**	10+ **4**	**6**	**1**
1− **6**	**5**	17+ **1**	**2**	**3**	3− **4**	**7**
4− **3**	**7**	**6**	**5**	**2**	5+ **1**	**4**

Puzzle 215

+ − × ÷

5− 6	1	3− 5	2	12× 3	4	15+ 7
2÷ 4	5− 2	13+ 6	1− 7	4− 1	5	3
2	7	3	6	12+ 4	6− 1	5
4− 1	5	4	9+ 3	2	7	6 6
15× 5	2− 4	8+ 7	1	6	24× 3	2
3	6	1	5	5− 7	2	4
10+ 7	3	2÷ 2	4	1− 5	6	1

Puzzle 216

+ − × ÷

12+ 2	3	24× 4	6	1	2− 7	5
1	6	13+ 7	180× 4	3	1− 5	2− 2
210× 7	1− 1	2	3	5	6	4
5	2	3	1 1	17+ 6	4	7
6	5 5	1	13+ 7	4	5+ 2	3÷ 3
336× 4	7	30× 6	5	2	3	1
3	4	70× 5	2	7	5− 1	6

Puzzle 217

+ − × ÷

84× 6	7	**10+** 2	3	5	**10+** 1	4
6+ 1	2	**18+** 3	4	6	5	**14+** 7
2	**18×** 3	4	**35×** 7	1	**168×** 6	5
3	1	6	5	7	4	2
10+ 4	6	**3−** 5	2	**3** 3	**6−** 7	1
140× 5	4	**84×** 7	1	2	**12+** 3	6
7	**6+** 5	1	6	**2÷** 4	2	3

Puzzle 218

+ − × ÷

7 7	**2−** 3	**2÷** 1	**70×** 5	**7+** 4	**12+** 6	2
2− 1	5	2	7	3	4	**1−** 6
3	**56×** 4	**2−** 6	2	**5−** 1	**13+** 5	7
2	7	4	**7+** 1	6	3	5
1− 5	**1−** 2	3	6	**6−** 7	1	**12×** 4
6	**6−** 1	7	**1−** 4	**9+** 5	2	3
2− 4	6	**5** 5	3	2	**8+** 7	1

Puzzle 219

+ − × ÷

105× 5	3	7	2÷ 4	2	13+ 6	5+ 1
6− 1	28× 7	7+ 3	1− 6	5	2	4
7	4	1	3	10+ 6	5	168× 2
7+ 2	5	6 6	16+ 7	1	4	3
12× 4	5− 6	5	2	3	11+ 1	7
3	1	2	9+ 5	4	7	1− 6
48× 6	2	4	8+ 1	7	3	5

Puzzle 220

+ − × ÷

6+ 1	5	72× 3	6	4	14× 2	7
4− 7	2÷ 4	10+ 6	1	2− 3	5	2÷ 2
3	2	4	18+ 7	5	6	1
2÷ 6	3	10× 5	5− 2	7	3− 1	4
1− 4	1− 7	2	15× 5	1	3	2÷ 6
5	6	1	84× 4	15+ 2	7	3
1− 2	1	7	3	6	1− 4	5

Puzzle 221

					+ − × ÷	
126× **7**	11+ **5**	**4**	2÷ **6**	**3**	2÷ **1**	**2**
6	**3**	**2**	20+ **7**	**5**	3− **4**	**1**
13+ **1**	**4**	**5**	**3**	84× **7**	4− **2**	**6**
1− **5**	**1**	12× **3**	**4**	**2**	90× **6**	7 **7**
4	**7**	14+ **1**	**2**	**6**	**3**	**5**
12× **3**	**2**	**6**	**5**	6+ **1**	14+ **7**	**4**
2	1− **6**	**7**	**1**	**4**	5 **5**	**3**

Puzzle 222

					+ − × ÷	
2− **6**	21× **7**	**1**	9+ **4**	**3**	1− **5**	3− **2**
4	**3**	3− **7**	2520× **1**	**2**	**6**	**5**
105× **3**	8+ **2**	**4**	**5**	**6**	224× **7**	1 **1**
7	**1**	**5**	**6**	**4**	**2**	21× **3**
5	24× **6**	1− **3**	**2**	**1**	**4**	**7**
2÷ **1**	**4**	**2**	**7**	15+ **5**	3÷ **3**	24× **6**
2	1− **5**	**6**	**3**	**7**	**1**	**4**

Puzzle 223

+ − × ÷

48× 3	4	9+ 1	3− 5	42× 6	6× 2	6− 7
4	5− 6	5	2	7	3	1
10× 5	1	3	14+ 7	2÷ 2	4	14+ 6
2	3− 7	4	1	3− 3	6	5
1	3− 2	15+ 7	6	1− 4	5	3
126× 6	5	2	1− 3	4− 1	8+ 7	2÷ 4
7	3	6	4	5	1	2

Puzzle 224

+ − × ÷

6× 3	19+ 1	7	5	3÷ 2	6	3− 4
2	8× 4	6	168× 7	8+ 3	5	1
1	2	4	6	18+ 7	8+ 3	5
42× 7	6	7+ 3	4	5	1− 1	2
420× 4	5	6+ 1	2	6	4− 7	3
11+ 5	7	8+ 2	3	3− 1	4	1− 6
6	3	5	1	2− 4	2	7

Puzzle 225

+ − × ÷

21× 7	3	14+ 1	6	2	1− 4	5
23+ 1	6	7	5	1− 3	2÷ 2	4
2	7	2− 3	1	4	9+ 5	84× 6
4 4	3− 2	5	2÷ 3	6	1	7
15+ 5	4	42× 6	7	6+ 1	3	2
6	3− 1	4	8+ 2	5	4− 7	3
2− 3	5	2	4	14+ 7	6	1

Puzzle 226

+ − × ÷

18× 1	3	15+ 7	10+ 4	6− 8	2	120× 5	6
36× 3	6	8	1	5	5− 7	2	4
2	200× 5	4− 4	8	3× 1	3	2− 6	7 7
6	8	5	21× 3	7	1	4	7+ 2
15+ 7	3+ 2	1 1	2÷ 6	3	2÷ 4	8	5
8	1	10× 2	5	24× 4	6	21× 7	3
4 4	140× 7	2÷ 3	5− 2	3÷ 6	13+ 5	7− 1	8
5	4	6	7	2	8	3÷ 3	1

Puzzle 227

+ − × ÷

24× 6	4	5− 7	7− 8	2− 5	3	2÷ 2	1
11+ 5	6	2	1	6+ 3	192× 4	8	12+ 7
28× 7	2÷ 8	4	2	1	6	3÷ 3	5
4	210× 7	5	6	17+ 8	2	1	2÷ 3
5− 8	1	1− 3	4	12× 2	7	11+ 5	6
3	3− 5	8	7 7	6	1	4	2
2÷ 1	2	3− 6	3	3− 4	20+ 5	7	192× 8
6× 2	3	4− 1	5	7	8	6	4

Puzzle 228

+ − × ÷

120× 6	4	56× 7	1	13+ 3	2	8	3− 5
5	21× 7	3	4	2	1− 6	2÷ 1	8
4− 3	7+ 6	1	18+ 5	8	7	2	2÷ 4
7	1	2÷ 4	8	5	2÷ 3	6	2
40× 1	3÷ 2	6	42× 7	2÷ 4	8	2− 5	3
8	5	80× 2	6	1	120× 4	21× 3	7
12× 4	3	8	1− 2	6	5	18+ 7	1
4÷ 2	8	5	8+ 3	7	1	4	6

Puzzle 229

+ − × ÷

2− **4**	10+ **3**	1− **7**	**6**	4÷ **2**	**8**	100× **1**	**5**
6	**2**	96× **8**	2− **3**	6− **1**	1− **7**	**5**	**4**
15× **1**	**4**	**2**	**5**	**7**	**6**	5− **3**	**8**
5	**1**	**6**	4− **4**	**8**	4− **3**	**7**	42× **2**
3	21+ **6**	6+ **4**	**1**	1− **5**	3− **2**	8 **8**	**7**
8	**7**	**1**	14× **2**	**4**	**5**	12+ **6**	**3**
15+ **2**	**8**	**5**	**7**	3÷ **3**	**1**	**4**	7+ **6**
2− **7**	**5**	5− **3**	**8**	2− **6**	**4**	**2**	**1**

Puzzle 230

+ − × ÷

2÷ **2**	6− **1**	5− **6**	3− **5**	**8**	**4**	2− **7**	105× **3**
4	**7**	**1**	2÷ **3**	14× **2**	**6**	**5**	4÷ **8**
2− **3**	**5**	12× **4**	**6**	**7**	**1**	160× **8**	**2**
14× **7**	**2**	**3**	4− **8**	1 **1**	**5**	**4**	1− **6**
1	12+ **3**	1− **7**	**4**	16+ **6**	**8**	**2**	**5**
5	**4**	**8**	42× **7**	**3**	**2**	7+ **6**	**1**
2− **6**	4÷ **8**	**2**	6+ **1**	**5**	4− **7**	**3**	3− **4**
8	1− **6**	**5**	10+ **2**	**4**	**3**	**1**	**7**

Puzzle 231

+ − × ÷

60× 4	3	5	18+ 6	7	6− 8	2	7− 1
2÷ 1	2	336× 7	4	5	1− 6	3÷ 3	8
3− 6	4÷ 8	2	3	4	5	1	210× 7
3	15+ 7	8	15+ 2	7− 1	12× 4	5	6
5− 2	4÷ 1	6	7	8	3	2÷ 4	3− 5
7	4	10+ 3	3− 5	5− 6	1	8	2
3− 5	6	1	8	6+ 3	9+ 2	3− 7	4
8	1− 5	4	1	2	7	2÷ 6	3

Puzzle 232

+ − × ÷

96× 8	2	40× 5	8+ 7	1	3	2− 4	2− 6
4÷ 4	6	8	1	2 2	5	630× 7	3
1	2− 3	168× 2	4	7	15+ 8	6	5
280× 5	1	6	3− 3	2÷ 8	7	2÷ 2	4
7	8	3	19+ 6	4	12+ 1	6+ 5	9+ 2
2 2	20× 5	28× 4	8	3	6	1	7
126× 3	4	7	5	1− 6	2	96× 8	7− 1
6	7	1− 1	2	5	4	3	8

Puzzle 233

+ − × ÷

126X 6	3	7	12+ 2	4	5 5	56X 8	1
20+ 5	20X 4	1	6	19+ 3	8	2	7
8	5	15+ 3	4	6− 7	6	2÷ 1	2
7	10X 2	5	8	1	48X 3	4	48X 6
4÷ 1	5− 6	30X 2	3	5	4	2− 7	8
4	1	1− 6	7	80X 8	14X 2	5	13+ 3
48X 3	15+ 7	8	5	2	1	6	4
2	8	11+ 4	1	6	7	2− 3	5

Puzzle 234

+ − × ÷

12X 4	16+ 8	1	7	30X 3	2	5	3÷ 6
3	21X 7	13+ 6	5	8+ 1	20+ 4	8	2
35X 7	3	2	1	6	8	4 4	3− 5
5	1	2÷ 3	6	3− 4	70X 7	2	8
11+ 2	4	192X 8	3	7	5	7+ 6	1
7− 1	5	18+ 7	2	2− 8	6	3÷ 3	3− 4
8	6	5	4	80X 2	3÷ 3	1	7
3÷ 6	2	4 4	8	5	1	4− 7	3

Puzzle 235

+ − × ÷

28× 4	7	2− 3	5	8+ 1	18+ 6	8	30× 2
21+ 7	8	6	2	5	4	6× 1	3
7− 8	2÷ 2	2÷ 4	4− 3	7	21× 1	6	5
1	4	8	10+ 6	4− 2	3	12+ 5	7
2÷ 2	1	490× 5	4	6	7	16+ 3	8
1− 5	6	2	7	5− 3	8	4	1
2÷ 6	2− 3	7	14+ 1	8	5	2÷ 2	4
3	5	1 1	2÷ 8	4	15+ 2	7	6

Puzzle 236

+ − × ÷

24× 2	13+ 1	4	15+ 7	1− 6	5	5− 8	3
4	3	8	1	7	24× 2	6	210× 5
3− 5	8	12× 3	4	16+ 1	7	2	6
16+ 3	6	1	2÷ 2	4	8	20× 5	7
2− 6	7	4÷ 2	8	2− 5	3÷ 3	4	12+ 1
8	11+ 2	180× 5	6	3	1	7	4
6− 7	5	6	1− 3	2	4 4	7− 1	8
1	4	20+ 7	5	8	36× 6	3	2

Puzzle 237

						+ − × ÷	
224X 8	4	7	3÷ 3	9+ 2	1	24+ 5	6
13+ 4	4− 7	2÷ 2	1	6X 3	6	2− 8	5
7	3	4	2	1	5 5	6	8
2	30X 1	2− 3	11+ 5	6	96X 8	4	3− 7
6	5	1	15+ 7	8	3	2÷ 2	4
2− 5	4− 6	192X 8	4	5− 7	2	1	6+ 3
3	2	6	3− 8	5	112X 4	4− 7	1
7− 1	8	1− 5	6	4	7	3	2

Puzzle 238

						+ − × ÷	
2 2	12X 3	4	20+ 5	1	7	48X 8	6
1− 3	4	8+ 5	7	4÷ 2	3÷ 6	5− 1	1− 8
12+ 5	1	3	4− 4	8	2	6	7
6	26+ 5	4÷ 2	8	3÷ 3	1	3− 7	4
4÷ 1	7	8	2− 3	2− 6	4	1− 2	5 5
4	6	15+ 7	1	9+ 5	11+ 8	3	2÷ 2
1− 7	8	6	2	4	3	12+ 5	1
8	2÷ 2	1	6 6	35X 7	5	4	3

Puzzle 239

+ − × ÷

1−		56×		2−		21+	
6	5	7	8	1	3	4	2
16+	1−	1−	2÷		3÷		
5	1	4	3	6	2	7	8
			13+	24×		1	6−
4	2	3	5	8	6	1	7
	4				13+		
7	4	2	6	3	8	5	1
7−	1−	24×		40×		120×	
1	7	6	4	2	5	8	3
		7−	5−		140×	11+	
8	6	1	2	4	7	3	5
16+						2−	
2	3	8	7	5	1	6	4
		6+		7			
3	8	5	1	7	4	2	6

Puzzle 240

+ − × ÷

10+	24×		12+	7−		2−	
2	4	6	3	8	1	7	5
		8+			2÷		7−
7	1	2	5	4	3	6	8
30×				9+	27+		
5	6	4	2	3	7	8	1
36×		5−					7
6	2	3	1	5	8	4	7
	2−		15+			1−	
1	3	8	6	7	2	5	4
		7	1−	2÷	10+	3÷	
3	5	7	8	1	4	2	6
19+	3−					3÷	
4	8	5	7	2	6	1	3
		4÷		1−		6×	
8	7	1	4	6	5	3	2

Puzzle 241

+ − × ÷

2	5	8	4	1	3	7	6
7	4	3	5	2	1	6	8
6	7	1	8	4	5	2	3
8	1	4	3	6	7	5	2
5	2	6	1	3	4	8	7
4	6	7	2	5	8	3	1
1	3	2	7	8	6	4	5
3	8	5	6	7	2	1	4

Puzzle 242

+ − × ÷

4	7	1	2	6	5	8	3
2	1	3	4	5	7	6	8
5	3	8	1	7	6	2	4
1	4	5	8	2	3	7	6
3	2	6	7	4	8	1	5
7	8	2	6	3	4	5	1
6	5	7	3	8	1	4	2
8	6	4	5	1	2	3	7

Puzzle 243

+ − × ÷

4− 7	17+ 8	9	6+ 5	12× 3	13+ 1	6	2 2	64× 4
3	16+ 9	7	1	4	6	5 5	8	2
20× 4	5	8+ 3	15+ 6	7	2	8− 1	54× 9	5− 8
3+ 1	2	5	224× 4	8	7	9	6	3
3÷ 6	252× 7	4	9	40× 5	8	5+ 2	3	54× 1
2	4 4	1− 8	7	8− 1	9	8+ 3	5	6
13+ 5	3+ 1	2	4÷ 8	18× 6	3	3− 4	7	9
8	2÷ 3	6	2	13+ 9	4	8+ 7	1	140× 5
15+ 9	6	3÷ 1	3	2 2	3− 5	8	4	7

Puzzle 244

+ − × ÷

360× 5	2	4	252× 9	7− 8	1	3 3	6	1− 7
9	1− 6	40× 8	7	10+ 1	2	4	3	90× 5
6× 6	7	5	4	5− 3	8	18+ 1	14× 2	9
1	72× 4	6	3	2− 9	9+ 5	8	7	2
6× 2	8+ 5	1	19+ 6	7	4	9	168× 8	3
3	8− 9	2	8	5	2÷ 6	7	1	4 4
2÷ 8	1	63× 7	8+ 5	4 4	3	60× 2	4− 9	2− 6
4	3 3	9	1	2	22+ 7	6	5	8
1− 7	8	1− 3	2	6	9	5	4÷ 4	1

Puzzle 245

+ − × ÷

8− 1	6 6	70× 7	5	2	5− 4	9	17+ 3	8
9	180× 3	2 2	12× 4	18+ 8	1	2− 7	5	6
5	2	6	3	9	1− 7	9+ 8	1	15+ 4
18+ 4	8	5	3÷ 9	3	6	5− 1	16+ 7	2
42× 7	1	120× 3	2	2÷ 4	8	6	9	5
3	5	4	13+ 6	7	4− 9	64× 2	8	1
2	2− 7	1− 9	7− 8	12+ 1	5	4	2− 6	3
2− 6	9	8	1	5	1− 2	3	4	126× 7
8	28× 4	1	7	6	2− 3	5	2	9

Puzzle 246

+ − × ÷

2÷ 1	2	35+ 5	6	9	8	7	4− 3	108× 4
3÷ 2	5− 6	224× 4	5− 3	8	4− 1	5	7	9
6	1	8	20× 7	3÷ 5	108× 2	4	9	3
3− 7	14+ 5	2	14+ 9	4	6	3	1	384× 8
4	7	8− 9	5	1− 2	3	14+ 1	8	6
216× 8	9	1	1− 2	3	7	6	100× 4	5
3	2÷ 8	6− 7	1	7+ 6	36× 4	9	5	14× 2
17+ 5	4	11+ 3	8	1	7− 9	2	3÷ 6	7
9	3	2− 6	4	2− 7	5	8 8	2	1

Puzzle 247

+ − × ÷

42× 6	270× 9	2	12+ 5	1 1	2÷ 4	4− 3	7	144× 8
1	5	3	7	5− 9	8	2÷ 4	2	6
7	448× 8	8− 1	9	4	13+ 2	5	6	3
8	7	18+ 6	7+ 4	3	18× 9	2	17+ 5	1
5 5	4	8	126× 3	6	7	8× 1	9	2
24× 4	6	21+ 9	32× 2	6+ 5	1	8	504× 3	2÷ 7
3	1	5	8	2	6	7	4	9
7− 2	3	21+ 7	6	8	105× 5	8− 9	1	1− 4
9	8× 2	4	1	7	3	2− 6	8	5

Puzzle 248

+ − × ÷

45× 3	5	10+ 1	2	7	5− 9	2− 6	8	3− 4
16× 2	3	23+ 5	8	6	4	8− 1	9	7
1	8	4	90× 5	1− 2	3	2− 9	7	16+ 6
11+ 5	19+ 7	3	6	4÷ 4	1	4÷ 8	2	9
4	2	9	3	1− 8	7	30× 5	6	1
21+ 8	4	7 7	8− 9	1	180× 6	2	3	5
42× 7	9	2− 6	252× 4	3− 5	8	1− 3	4− 1	6× 2
6	1	8	7	210× 9	2	4	5	3
108× 9	6	2	1	3	5	7	2÷ 4	8

Puzzle 249

+ − × ÷

3÷ 6	12× 4	3	4− 5	1− 2	576× 9	8	2− 7	36× 1
2	1− 6	7	1	3	8	9 9	5	4
840× 3	5	8	7	3÷ 6	2	4÷ 4	1	9
3− 7	7− 1	1− 2	7− 9	9+ 4	2÷ 3	240× 5	8	6
4	8	1	2	5	6	3÷ 3	9	14+ 7
5 5	2÷ 3	6	18+ 8	9	1	84× 7	4	2
2÷ 1	2	13+ 9	4	280× 8	7	5− 6	3	5
504× 8	36× 9	4	13+ 6	7	5	1	4− 2	5− 3
9	7	15+ 5	3	1	4	2	6	8

Puzzle 250

+ − × ÷

24+ 2	1568× 7	8	9+ 6	1	5 5	14+ 9	1− 4	3
8	4	7	8− 1	2	12× 6	5	3÷ 3	9
5	2÷ 3	6	9	3456× 8	2	1	140× 7	4
9	3÷ 2	18+ 4	8	6	3÷ 1	3	5	12+ 7
18+ 3	6	2	4	9	8	14× 7	1	5
6	9	15× 5	3	196× 4	7	2÷ 8	2	2÷ 1
280× 1	8	13+ 9	210× 5	7	144× 3	4	29+ 6	2
7	5	1	2	3	4	6	9	8 8
4÷ 4	1	3	7	4− 5	9	2	8	6

Puzzle 251

+ − × ÷

1− **3**	2÷ **8**	**4**	20X **5**	26+ **7**	**6**	1512X **9**	2÷ **2**	**1**
2	4− **5**	**9**	**1**	**6**	**4**	**7**	**8**	**3**
18+ **8**	8− **9**	**1**	**4**	**3**	42X **7**	**6**	18+ **5**	**2**
6	1− **1**	189X **3**	**9**	10+ **5**	6− **8**	**2**	**7**	**4**
4	**2**	**7**	5− **3**	**1**	9 **9**	240X **8**	**6**	**5**
1− **7**	**6**	60X **5**	**8**	**4**	2÷ **2**	**1**	20+ **3**	**9**
1260X **9**	**4**	**2**	**6**	72X **8**	8+ **3**	**5**	**1**	**7**
5	**7**	2− **6**	9+ **2**	**9**	**1**	16+ **3**	4− **4**	**8**
3÷ **1**	**3**	**8**	3− **7**	**2**	**5**	**4**	**9**	6 **6**

Puzzle 252

+ − × ÷

11+ **1**	280X **5**	**7**	20+ **4**	160X **8**	7− **9**	1− **6**	3− **3**	2÷ **2**
3	**7**	**8**	**9**	**4**	**2**	**5**	**6**	**1**
48X **8**	6X **3**	30X **6**	**7**	**5**	36X **4**	**1**	2÷ **2**	35+ **9**
6	**2**	**5**	**1**	11+ **3**	**8**	**9**	**4**	**7**
13+ **7**	4− **4**	13+ **2**	**5**	15+ **6**	17+ **1**	16+ **3**	**9**	**8**
2	**8**	3÷ **3**	**6**	**9**	**7**	**4**	8+ **1**	**5**
4	8− **1**	**9**	1− **8**	**7**	**3**	**2**	**5**	**6**
4− **5**	**9**	24X **1**	1− **3**	1− **2**	**6**	224X **7**	**8**	**4**
9	**6**	**4**	**2**	**1**	40X **5**	**8**	4− **7**	**3**

Puzzle 253

+ − × ÷

504X 7	5− 3	120X 4	6	7− 8	8− 9	1	14+ 5	2
9	8	3÷ 2	5	1	3÷ 3	2÷ 4	14+ 6	7
8	12+ 7	6	5− 4	9	1	2	3	5
1	5	22+ 9	7	6	14X 2	3÷ 3	4÷ 4	4− 8
360X 2	6	5	5− 8	3	7	9	1	4
6	12X 4	3	7− 9	64X 2	8	2− 5	7	10+ 1
21X 3	1	7	2	4	3− 5	8	756X 9	6
180X 4	9	7− 8	1	105X 5	6	7	2	3
5	2÷ 2	1	3	7	2− 4	6	17+ 8	9

Puzzle 254

+ − × ÷

1− 7	2÷ 4	8	60X 6	2	3÷ 3	9	4− 5	1
8	1323X 7	9	5− 4	5	2÷ 2	10+ 6	1	3
1− 5	3	7	9	2− 6	4	11+ 1	8	2
4	45X 5	13+ 6	7	8	3÷ 1	3	24X 2	30+ 9
18X 2	9	1	2÷ 8	4	14+ 7	5	3	6
9	11+ 6	5	3÷ 1	3	2− 8	2	4	7
2X 1	2	20+ 3	5	7	6	288X 4	9	8
2÷ 6	1	2	3	8− 9	4− 5	8	28X 7	4
3	8 8	2÷ 4	2	1	9	18+ 7	6	5

Puzzle 255

+ − × ÷

3÷ 3	2÷ 8	4	3÷ 1	2− 6	70X 7	2	4− 5	9
9	7+ 1	6	3	4	15+ 8	5	2 2	56X 7
5− 4	9	15+ 8	6	1	5	5− 3	42X 7	2
1− 5	6	126X 9	7	20+ 3	2	8	1	4
56X 7	4	2	5	9	3	8− 1	6	144X 8
1	2	15+ 7	8	3− 5	252X 4	9	5− 3	6
144X 6	20X 5	1	4	2	9	7	8	3
8	3	10+ 5	2	1− 7	6	144X 4	9	4− 1
5− 2	7	3	18+ 9	8	1	6 6	4	5

Puzzle 256

+ − × ÷

48X 4	6	2	96X 3	8	8− 9	10+ 7	1− 1	3− 5
14+ 9	5	3− 6	4	168X 7	1	3	2	8
1134X 6	7	9	4− 5	4	13+ 8	1	1− 3	2
3	9	5 5	1	6	4	128X 2	8	315X 7
28X 1	4	7	11+ 6	3	2	8	5	9
3− 5	6+ 2	3	4÷ 8	10+ 1	3− 6	9	14+ 7	4
8	1	16+ 4	2	9	10+ 7	1− 5	6	3
17+ 2	8	1	12+ 7	5	3	2− 4	5− 9	7+ 6
7	3	8	90X 9	2	5	6	4	1

Puzzle 257

+ − × ÷

63X		4÷	48X	360X			7+	
7	9	1	8	6	5	2	3	4
144X	3			8X		2−	6+	
9	3	4	2	8	6	7	1	5
		1−			14+		60X	2÷
2	4	7	3	1	8	9	5	6
2÷			2−					
4	2	8	9	7	1	5	6	3
	12+			13+	1−			7−
8	5	3	4	9	7	6	2	1
2÷		4−	14+		5−	6−		
3	6	2	5	4	9	1	7	8
6+						20+		
5	1	6	7	2	4	3	8	9
7+	24+		1−		24X		5−	14X
1	7	9	6	5	3	8	4	2
		15+						
6	8	5	1	3	2	4	9	7

Puzzle 258

+ − × ÷

12X		4−	2÷	1−		14+		14+
3	4	9	2	8	7	1	6	5
3−	1−		8−					
2	8	5	4	1	9	7	3	6
		5−		9	72X	2−	2÷	
5	7	3	8	9	4	6	2	1
23+	1−		70X				3÷	
9	5	4	7	2	6	8	1	3
	4÷					21+		3−
6	2	8	1	5	3	9	7	4
	5−		4−	9+				
8	1	6	9	4	2	3	5	7
11+	1−			5−		64X	648X	
7	3	2	5	6	1	4	9	8
	6	6−	19+		18+			
4	6	1	3	7	5	2	8	9
10+						2÷		
1	9	7	6	3	8	5	4	2

Puzzle 259

+ − × ÷

1− **8**	3÷ **9**	1− **2**	**3**	35× **5**	**7**	2÷ **1**	30× **6**	10+ **4**
9	**3**	256× **4**	**8**	23+ **7**	**1**	**2**	**5**	**6**
11+ **6**	**5**	**8**	**4**	**3**	**9**	4− **7**	2÷ **1**	**2**
4− **1**	256× **4**	30+ **7**	**9**	**6**	**8**	**3**	16+ **2**	**5**
5	**8**	630× **3**	**7**	8− **1**	48× **2**	**6**	**4**	**9**
4	**2**	**5**	**6**	**9**	96× **3**	**8**	7 **7**	16+ **1**
10+ **3**	6 **6**	54× **9**	1− **1**	**2**	14+ **5**	**4**	**8**	**7**
7	10+ **1**	**6**	14+ **2**	**8**	**4**	**5**	6− **9**	**3**
2	**7**	6+ **1**	**5**	**4**	3− **6**	**9**	5− **3**	**8**

Business/Accounting & Bookkeeping

Bookkeeping
For Dummies
978-0-7645-9848-7

eBay Business
All-in-One
For Dummies,
2nd Edition
978-0-470-38536-4

Job Interviews
For Dummies,
3rd Edition
978-0-470-17748-8

Resumes For Dummies,
5th Edition
978-0-470-08037-5

Stock Investing
For Dummies,
3rd Edition
978-0-470-40114-9

Successful Time
Management
For Dummies
978-0-470-29034-7

Computer Hardware

BlackBerry
For Dummies,
3rd Edition
978-0-470-45762-7

Computers For Seniors
For Dummies
978-0-470-24055-7

iPhone For Dummies,
2nd Edition
978-0-470-42342-4

Laptops For Dummies,
3rd Edition
978-0-470-27759-1

Macs For Dummies,
10th Edition
978-0-470-27817-8

Cooking & Entertaining

Cooking Basics
For Dummies,
3rd Edition
978-0-7645-7206-7

Wine For Dummies,
4th Edition
978-0-470-04579-4

Diet & Nutrition

Dieting For Dummies,
2nd Edition
978-0-7645-4149-0

Nutrition For Dummies,
4th Edition
978-0-471-79868-2

Weight Training
For Dummies,
3rd Edition
978-0-471-76845-6

Digital Photography

Digital Photography
For Dummies,
6th Edition
978-0-470-25074-7

Photoshop Elements 7
For Dummies
978-0-470-39700-8

Gardening

Gardening Basics
For Dummies
978-0-470-03749-2

Organic Gardening
For Dummies,
2nd Edition
978-0-470-43067-5

Green/Sustainable

Green Building
& Remodeling
For Dummies
978-0-4710-17559-0

Green Cleaning
For Dummies
978-0-470-39106-8

Green IT For Dummies
978-0-470-38688-0

Health

Diabetes For Dummies,
3rd Edition
978-0-470-27086-8

Food Allergies
For Dummies
978-0-470-09584-3

Living Gluten-Free
For Dummies
978-0-471-77383-2

Hobbies/General

Chess For Dummies,
2nd Edition
978-0-7645-8404-6

Drawing For Dummies
978-0-7645-5476-6

Knitting For Dummies,
2nd Edition
978-0-470-28747-7

Organizing For Dummies
978-0-7645-5300-4

SuDoku For Dummies
978-0-470-01892-7

Home Improvement

Energy Efficient Homes
For Dummies
978-0-470-37602-7

Home Theater
For Dummies,
3rd Edition
978-0-470-41189-6

Living the Country
Lifestyle
All-in-One For Dummies
978-0-470-43061-3

Solar Power Your Home
For Dummies
978-0-470-17569-9

Internet

Blogging For Dummies,
2nd Edition
978-0-470-23017-6

eBay For Dummies,
6th Edition
978-0-470-49741-8

Facebook For Dummies
978-0-470-26273-3

Google Blogger
For Dummies
978-0-470-40742-4

Web Marketing
For Dummies,
2nd Edition
978-0-470-37181-7

WordPress
For Dummies,
2nd Edition
978-0-470-40296-2

Language & Foreign Language

French For Dummies
978-0-7645-5193-2

Italian Phrases
For Dummies
978-0-7645-7203-6

Spanish For Dummies
978-0-7645-5194-9

Spanish For Dummies,
Audio Set
978-0-470-09585-0

Macintosh

Mac OS X Snow Leopard
For Dummies
978-0-470-43543-4

Math & Science

Algebra I For Dummies
978-0-7645-5325-7

Biology For Dummies
978-0-7645-5326-4

Calculus For Dummies
978-0-7645-2498-1

Chemistry For Dummies
978-0-7645-5430-8

Microsoft Office

Excel 2007 For Dummies
978-0-470-03737-9

Office 2007
All-in-One
Desk Reference
For Dummies
978-0-471-78279-7

Music

Guitar For Dummies,
2nd Edition
978-0-7645-9904-0

iPod & iTunes
For Dummies,
6th Edition
978-0-470-39062-7

Piano Exercises
For Dummies
978-0-470-38765-8

Parenting & Education

Parenting For Dummies,
2nd Edition
978-0-7645-5418-6

Type 1 Diabetes
For Dummies
978-0-470-17811-9

Pets

Cats For Dummies,
2nd Edition
978-0-7645-5275-5

Dog Training
For Dummies,
2nd Edition
978-0-7645-8418-3

Puppies For Dummies,
2nd Edition
978-0-470-03717-1

Religion & Inspiration

The Bible For Dummies
978-0-7645-5296-0

Catholicism
For Dummies
978-0-7645-5391-2

Women in the Bible
For Dummies
978-0-7645-8475-6

Self-Help & Relationship

Anger Management
For Dummies
978-0-470-03715-7

Overcoming Anxiety
For Dummies
978-0-7645-5447-6

Sports

Baseball For Dummies,
3rd Edition
978-0-7645-7537-2

Basketball For
Dummies,
2nd Edition
978-0-7645-5248-9

Golf For Dummies,
3rd Edition
978-0-471-76871-5

Web Development

Web Design All-in-One
For Dummies
978-0-470-41796-6

Windows Vista

Windows Vista
For Dummies
978-0-471-75421-3

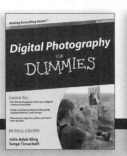